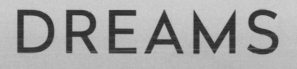

DREAMS

A CONSCIOUS GUIDE

TREE CARR

DREAMS

How to connect with your dreams
to enrich your life

aster

Dedicated to Ren

An Hachette UK Company
www.hachette.co.uk

First published in Great Britain in 2018 by Aster, an imprint of
Octopus Publishing Group Ltd
Carmelite House
50 Victoria Embankment
London EC4Y 0DZ
www.octopusbooks.co.uk

Distributed in the US by
Hachette Book Group
1290 Avenue of the Americas
4th and 5th Floors
New York, NY 10104

Distributed in Canada by
Canadian Manda Group,
664 Annette St., Toronto,
Ontario, Canada M6S 2C8

ISBN 9781912023967

A CIP catalogue record for this book is available from the British Library.

Printed and bound in China

10 9 8 7 6 5 4 3 2 1

Consultant Publisher: Kate Adams
Senior Editor: Pollyanna Poulter
Copy Editor: Theresa Bebbington
Art Director: Juliette Norsworthy
Design and Illustration: Ella McLean
Production Manager: Lisa Pinnell

Disclaimer/Publisher's note
All reasonable care has been taken in the preparation of this book but the
information it contains is not intended to take the place of treatment by
a qualified medical practitioner.

Before making any changes in your health regime, always consult a doctor.
While all the practices detailed in this book are completely safe if done
correctly, you must seek professional advice if you are in any doubt about
any medical condition. Any application of the ideas and information
contained in this book is at the reader's sole discretion and risk.

Contents

Introduction

Dreaming is the exploration of your own consciousness.

You have the ability to have an enriching and more connected
dream life – one that is filled with flying, adventure, creativity,
magic, possibility, love, insight, guidance and transcendence.
You have the possibility to explore your own consciousness and
all the wonderful mysteries that it encounters as you dream.
You also have the opportunity to carry these dreams through
into your waking life to produce a positive effect on your life,
the lives of others and the world around you.

Conscious dreaming practice

In this introductory book, I will guide you through the
conscious dreaming practice that I've cultivated over
the past few decades. Much like yoga and meditation,
it is a practice that can be implemented in your daily life.

Through a combination of intent, mindfulness, reflection,
record-keeping, plant care and lifestyle changes, you will
find yourself connecting more deeply to the mysteries
of your consciousness as you sleep. You will also find that
this new connectedness brings a greater richness, magic,
creativity and purpose into your waking life.

I will guide you through the science of sleep, the core
foundations of my conscious dreaming practice, dream
plants and herbs, and dream genres. I will also share with
you my personal experiences from my own dreaming life,
as well as provide lots of useful tips on how to harness
your own conscious dreaming practice.

Who benefits from conscious dream practice?

My conscious dreaming practice is for everyone. If you are a human being and you dream, then it is for you. No matter what your belief system is, this practice can be used alongside it. If you are atheist, religious, spiritual, scientific, agnostic, it does not make a difference. All you need is the belief in your own consciousness. However, you will also need some discipline – what we practise, we get good at.

This guide will help illustrate how, as a conscious dreamer, you can live a more lucid and aware waking life and how consciousness does not "stop" as soon as you lay your head down on a pillow. It continues through dreaming and it can be enriching, healing and inspiring enough to continue into your waking life.

By embracing my conscious dreaming practice, you will not only wake up to your dreams, you will wake up to YOU.

Dreaming and consciousness

It's amazing to consider how entire populations of people lay their head down on their pillow every night and fall into stillness and silence. As they all slip under, their consciousness hovers in the liminal and strange threshold between wakefulness and sleep. They relax, shut down and dissolve into an altered state, and eventually they fall asleep and enter into the unknown.

A life filled with dreams

Every single one of us experiences dreaming whether or not we remember them. You begin dreaming at infancy and will continue until the day you die. You will spend about one-third of your life asleep and dreaming. This equates to approximately 25 years of engaging in your dreamworlds. Imagine exploring 25 years of an unknown aspect of yourself. A lot can get done!

Your dreams play out differently from your waking realities. In your dreamworlds, you may seem to be your usual self in surreal environments, or you may appear as aspects of yourself or even someone completely different. Dreams can certainly be entertaining, absurd, inspiring or frightening. You can experience a wide range of emotions, and upon awakening it can feel as though you really were there.

Dreams can often stay with you throughout the day and affect your mood and thinking. However, for the most part, you will probably shrug off your dreams and pay little attention to them.

Universal importance

Human beings have a long history of looking to their dreams for guidance, inspiration, spiritual connection and decision-making. Kings consulted seers or gifted dreamers for political advice, and tribe leaders took heed from the prophetic dreams of their shamans. Dreams have led to inventions and scientific discoveries as well as the creation of emotional works of music and art. There are many examples and references in a wide variety of cultures throughout history that illustrate the importance of dreams. From ancient Indian writings to Greek philosophers and onward, humanity has been intrigued enough by dreams to ensure that they were documented, while some other cultures passed on their dreaming traditions through both word of mouth and folklore.

In all of the unique ways that the importance of dreaming has evolved, it is safe to say that all humans can relate to the act of dreaming. It is a common and innately human experience that links us all together. We are able to bond with each other over the shared emotive power of a nightmare or the profound, exhilarating experience of a lucid dream.

I often see boundaries such as culture, age, race and gender dissolve when I hold my conscious dreaming retreats, workshops or dreaming circles. After everyone in the circle has shared a dream, there is almost a collective sigh of relief after the realization that we are all experiencing similar things. We are not alone in this.

Disconnection in the modern world

So why are modern humans so disconnected from their dreams? In an age of rampant industrialized consumerism and technological alienation, it seems that people are becoming disconnected from aspects of their inner worlds. Their quiet, reflective consciousness has been superseded by the noisy and distracted components of a modern, consumerist culture. They are also experiencing a disconnect from the natural world. They are spending tremendous amounts of time engaging with electronic devices and less time going for walks through fields or sitting in parks.

Even when they are walking through fields or sitting in parks, they have their smartphones with them, documenting their way through the entire experience on social media. They have lost their ability to be present, inward-focussed and reflective and have replaced it with a new habit of consciously projecting their immediate experiences outward to the world for validation. They have quickly lost the habit of taking time to stop and smell the roses; now they are too busy taking pictures of the roses!

These new habits of disconnection impact their abilities to connect to the reflective and deep nature of their minds and their dreams.

Consciousness through dreaming

I believe that dreams are experiences of consciousness. If you are alive, you experience consciousness. It is your personal awareness and perception of your reality, environment and experiences. It encompasses your senses, emotions, sensations and thoughts. Most would think that consciousness is what you are experiencing when you are awake, but there is much more to it. Consciousness can also be experienced through dreams, memories, comas, trance states, daydreams and psychedelic experiences. These types of experiences are coined as "altered states of consciousness" because they do not align with the definition of an awake, pragmatic and sober state of perception. They are, however, valid forms of consciousness because they fall within the experience of perception.

Even when you are asleep, your consciousness is still present; you are just unaware of it. The experience of the scenes unfolding in your dreams is just as wonderful, valid or important as anything you experience in waking life. In other words, just because dreams are "not real" does not mean you cannot feel like you experienced something real. For an advanced or lucid dreamer, their consciousness is present and aware within their dream. Even when asleep and dreaming, you have the ability to be aware and present with what is unfolding. You can be effectively "awake" in your dreams.

Practising conscious dreaming

By engaging in a committed conscious dreaming practice, you can train your mind to become more aware in a dream state, to be more fully engaged in your dreams, to begin to control your dreams and to decode their cryptic messages. This can, in return, awaken the dormant aspect of your consciousness and ignite potential vivid and rich dreaming states. You can then begin to completely engage in your dreams and use them for inspiration, emotional healing, problem-solving, entertainment and soul growth – and the list goes on. Every human being out there can dream, and through simple intent, mindfulness, reflection, record-keeping, plant care and lifestyle changes, you can enable a deeper connectivity and understanding of the profound mysteries that your consciousness experiences as you sleep. Come and join the exploration!

My story

For as long as I can remember, I have been fascinated by my dreams. My persistent experiences with sleep paralysis, precognitive and lucid dreams had profound effects on me that have led to a lifetime of exploration into their meaning.

Early childhood memories

I was a child in the 1970s and spent my young formative years living in a communal setting. There was no television or radio for my young mind to engage with. In fact, the first television I ever saw was when I was around six years old at a relative's house. I thought it was a toy that made moving pictures.

I spent a lot of time as a child engaging with my natural surroundings, I was often surrounded by music and had time to focus on my own mind. As a result, my dream life was vivid. Some of my earliest childhood memories are of my dreams. I can recall dreams from when I was as young as three years old: dreams about flying, falling down from outer space, the natural world, far-off lands and recurring dreams of soldiers, cowboys, Jesus Christ, giant robots, the moon, the ocean, angels, natural disasters and the end of the word.

Developing an interest in dreams

As I grew up, my exploration led to my recognition of the great potential of dreams. I began to view my dreams as worlds and thought forms that were just as valid as those of my waking life, and I made a decision to commit to a dream practice to further understand them and myself. As a teenager I began experiencing precognitive dreams, and my experiences with sleep paralysis became more intense. These prompted me to begin recording my dreams in a dream journal. This enabled me to process, interpret and analyse my dream experiences and the activity of my unconscious mind. It also helped me to keep records of my dreams so that I could look back and reflect upon them.

During these teenage years, my dreams also became a great inspiration for my creative life. I began to depict my experiences of sleep paralysis through my artwork. I would sketch, draw, paint and make collages. My favourite creative tool was an old black-and-white photocopier. I used to photocopy my face in movement as the machine scanned across my expressions, capturing them and spitting the results out on paper. This effect created menacing self-portraits of what I felt represented the feeling I experienced when being trapped in terrifying sleep paralysis while in dream states.

Benefits of dream journaling

Dream journaling helped me to categorize the different dream genres I was experiencing. I discovered that I was having a variety of dreams: lucid, compensatory, recurring, precognitive, symbolic, mutual and after-death visitation dreams, as well as sleep paralysis. Knowing that I could name the genre of dream that I had helped me to navigate my experiences. The process also helped me to integrate these experiences into my waking life. I began to bridge things that I learned, experienced and was inspired by from my dreams into my day-to-day reality. Whether it was creative motivation, personal guidance, guidance for others or just exploration, I allowed myself to work in partnership with my dreams so that I could grow and evolve as a person and explore the mystery of my own consciousness.

Through my personal journey I began to use my dreams for many different things: soul growth, emotional healing, creative inspiration, guidance, adventure, pleasure, problem-solving and helping others. Part of this journey led to my exploration of inducing lucid dreams.

Becoming a dream explorer

It was during these lucid dreaming teenage years that I began to speak more openly to my friends about my dreaming experiences. My good friend Ren (who recently left this realm much too soon) was a pivotal part of my evolution as an oneironaut. An oneironaut is a dream explorer – from the Greek words *oneiros* ("dream") and *nautes* ("sailor") – and Ren was a prolific oneironaut.

Ren and I would share with each other our lucid dream experiences, we experimented with methods and techniques, and sought out dreaming aids and herbs. We often appeared in each other's dreams and would let each other know if we had. We would share and brainstorm theories, personal insight, entertain cosmic possibilities and nerd out over anything and everything dreaming. This carried on for more than 27 years until Ren himself flew off into the great mystery.

A COMFORTING LUCID DREAM

Ren's abrupt death did not come without its foreshadowing. A couple of months before he drowned, he emailed me about a lucid dream he had about being in the ocean and getting sucked down into a vortex. I was with him, deep down in the ocean, and he was panicking. However, he saw that I was laughing and breathing underwater. This made him relax and start to laugh and breathe, too.

He then recounted that he was suddenly floating above the ocean and could see down into the vortex where he and I were. He was hovering above, observing himself with me, deep in the water vortex below. He began waving his arms to get our attention. We saw him and waved back from our watery place in the vortex. Ren's precognitive dream left an impression on me and it also, oddly, brought me great comfort when I reread it after he was found in the Pacific Ocean.

Sharing my dreaming practice

Ren's death woke up my internal dream machine and I began sharing my dreams with the external. This involved posting my dream journal entries online, making films about dreaming, and facilitating lucid dreaming retreats, workshops and dreaming circles.
I realized that my exploration and accumulative experience of my own conscious dreaming practice from the past 30 years had given me some knowledge to pass on. In a way, I feel like I'm keeping my dream inspiration and exploration relationship with Ren alive and evolving, except now I've stepped out into the bigger picture to share them with the world.

As a consciousness explorer, I do not subscribe to any religion or dogma. I see consciousness as an evolutionary work in progress and I do not see myself as having all the answers. As an explorer, I keep my mind open to wonder, open to change and excited by new possibilities and the territory of the unknown. I do not shut down my exploration because it has "not been proven by science". I embrace it, flow with it, evolve with it and I do not forget to laugh alongside it.

Through engaging in my conscious dreaming practice, I realized that my ability to be aware, engaged, informed and lucid within dream states has helped with the evolution of my expansion of consciousness. This has given me new ways of seeing reality in all its forms and degrees of intensity as well as a sense of wonder at the simple fact of just being alive.

Tonight, as you drift off to sleep, you can count sheep – or you can get ready for a journey into the unknown. With one-third of your life spent in the dreaming zone, you have plenty of time for dream exploration. I hope you feel inspired to join in and explore.

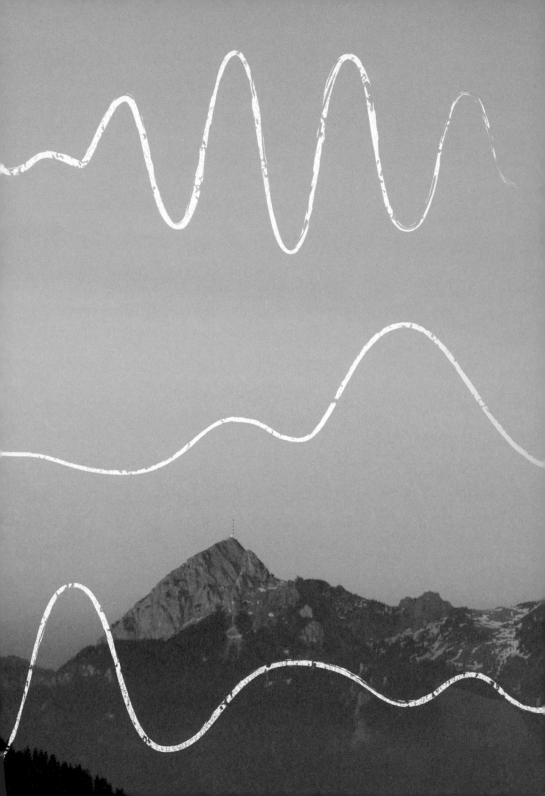

PART 1

The Science of Sleep

Introducing the science of sleep

Before embracing the conscious dreaming practice, it is helpful
to be of aware of and understand the physical and biological
aspects of sleeping and dreaming time. Sleep serves a function.
It exists to help maintain the physical and mental health of
a living being, and as a result it can improve the quality of life.

While you sleep, your body and brain go through several
integral processes that assist in your overall physical health
and mind function. Your brain processes information and
forms new pathways. These help you to learn and focus,
and they help your decision-making processes and memory.

THE HEALTH BENEFITS OF SLEEP

* MEMORY: during sleep, your brain strengthens your memories and the skills you have learned during your waking time.

* MOOD: a good sleep will help to reduce levels of stress, decrease irritability, and reduce emotional instability and depression.

* DEXTERITY: sleeplessness affects reaction times and decision-making. If you have healthy sleep, the chances of physically hurting yourself through accidents or clumsiness are reduced.

* WEIGHT: studies show that lack of proper sleep affects body weight. Sleep affects our endocrine system and hormones; if we do not get enough sleep, our metabolism changes and we can put on weight.

* MENTAL CLARITY: lack of sleep can result in symptoms similar to those of attention deficit hyperactivity disorder (ADHD), such as not being able to focus.

* LONGEVITY: too little sleep is associated with a shorter lifespan.

* STAMINA: studies show that athletes who sleep up to ten hours a night for seven to eight weeks have more stamina, less daytime fatigue and improve their average sprint time.

* PRODUCTIVITY: studies show that sleep deprivation impairs learning. Students who suffer sleep debt have been proven to have poorer grades than those who have adequate sleep.

* HEART: it is believed that inadequate sleep affects cholesterol levels, which is directly related to heart disease.

* ANTI-INFLAMMATORY: research indicates that inflammation is linked to stroke, heart disease, diabetes and premature ageing. Studies show that people who sleep for less than six hours per night have higher blood levels of inflammatory proteins than those who sleep for longer.

So now that we know why it's biologically important for us to sleep every night, let's have a look at the stages of sleep we can expect to go through on average when we fall asleep.

The stages of sleep

Understanding and navigating your stages of sleep can assist you in conscious dreaming. As you drift off, you normally go through several cycles of sleep. Within each cycle there are customarily five sleep stages.

The average sleep cycle lasts about 90 minutes and is repeated four to six times as you sleep. During those 90 minutes, we move through five stages of sleep. The first four stages make up our non-rapid eye movement (NREM) sleep, which form an average of 75 per cent of our sleep. It is sometimes referred to as quiet sleep. The fifth stage is when rapid eye movement (REM) sleep occurs, which makes up an average of 25 per cent of our sleep. During a normal sleep cycle, there are also brief 1–2-minute periods of waking. Bear in mind that the lengths of time of these various stages fluctuate with age, so a baby's sleep cycles, for example, will not be the same as those of an adult.

THE DISCOVERY OF REM

The REM state was discovered in 1953 by Eugene Aserinsky and Nathaniel Kleitman, US pioneers in sleep research. They noticed that when subjects were woken from sleep during the phase of sleep characterized by "rapid, jerky and binocularly symmetrical eye movements", they recalled the most vivid and elaborate dreams. When subjects were woken from non-REM sleep, however, significantly fewer dreams were reported, and the reports were less intense and more like memories of dreams. And so, the REM state was named and has been associated with dreaming ever since. Following the discovery of REM sleep, researchers concluded that there are three basic states of consciousness: wakefulness, REM sleep and NREM sleep.

STAGE ONE

ALSO KNOWN AS N1

Dozy

* *Between being awake and
  falling asleep*
* *Light sleep*

This stage is the transition between
wakefulness and sleep, when we find
ourselves drowsy and dozing off. It is
a NREM state in which you will feel
slightly awake as your drift in and out.
This phase of drowsiness usually lasts
1–10 minutes and leads into a light sleep.
This is the stage of the sleep cycle
where you may experience hypnagogia
(*see* The hypnagogic state, page 22),
muscle jerks and falling sensations.
There are varying theories about why
muscles jerk and people experience
these falling sensations: increased
physical activity or exercise in the
evening, anxiety, fatigue, stress,
caffeine, sleep deprivation, misfiring
of nerves and ancient primate reflexes.

Hypnagogic state

In the stage one phase of your sleep cycle, you will enter the hypnagogic state (from the Greek *hypnos*, for "sleep", and *agogos*, for "leading") immediately before falling asleep. During this transition from wakefulness to sleep, you can experience some interesting phenomena such as imagery, sounds and unusual sensations in the body. Not many people are able to remember the hypnagogic imagery that they experience. This phase sometimes lasts only a few seconds and is so fleeting that people are unaware of it. The startling nature of this ephemeral episode can occasionally jolt you awake, enabling you to remember the experience. But for the most part, you will not observe the hypnagogic state and will slip straight into sleep.

Those who do recall it report experiences of trippy visuals, sacred geometry and quick flashes of people's faces or everyday scenes. Other phenomena include auditory hallucinations: random snippets of people talking, mechanical sounds, electrical buzzes and rushing sounds. Some people hear their names being called, a baby crying or someone laughing loudly. And yet others will hear a piece of music, as if there is a full symphony orchestra in their bedroom.

Whenever I experience or observe my hypnagogic state, I liken it to my brain tuning into a radio station or television channel. It is fascinating to hold onto my awareness and be able to tune in and out of the visual and auditory events of this liminal state.

Many inventors, artists and scientists have reported having a "Eureka!" moment during a hypnagogic state. Thomas Edison and Salvador Dali both used methods in which they incubated hypnagogic dreams on purpose.

Hypnopompic state

Immediately before waking up, you enter the hypnopompic state (from the Greek *hypnos*, for "sleep", and *pompē*, for "sending away"). Similar to the hypnagogic state, it is also accompanied by all sorts of visual, sensory and auditory occurrences.

Imagine sensing that you are slowly transitioning from a sleeping state to being fully awake, when at some point during that transition you begin seeing vivid geometric shapes, hearing sounds or even sensing touch. These sensations could be described as hypnopompic in that you are not fully asleep, yet simultaneously you are not fully awake. Although hypnopompic phenomena are often reported among those with various types of sleep disorders (such as narcolepsy), they are also reported by 6.6 per cent of the general population. In some cases, these hypnopompic hallucinations can be frightening and accompanied by an episode of sleep paralysis (*see* page 126).

STAGE TWO

ALSO KNOWN AS N2

Light sleep
* *Onset of sleep*
* *Becoming disengaged from surroundings*

This lighter stage of sleep is also a NREM phase and lasts about 20 minutes. About 50 per cent of your time asleep is spent in stage two. During this stage, your breathing and heart rate are regular but your heart rate starts to slow down, your eye movement stops and your body temperature decreases (which is why sleeping in a cool room will help you fall asleep). Your brain waves begin to slow down, but there are occasional bursts of waves known as sleep spindles because of how they look on an electroencephalographic (EEG) reading. They appear as punctuated, voltage fluctuations, suggesting that there is something going on in the brain, such as a transfer of electrical energy.

STAGES THREE AND FOUR

ALSO KNOWN AS N3
(In 2008, the sleep profession
eliminated the use of stage four;
stages three and four are now
considered stage three or N3.)

Deep sleep
* *Deepest sleep stage*

Stages three and four are now often
coupled together because they are the
intervals of slow-wave sleep (SWS). As
your body moves from stage three to
stage four, the number of delta waves
in the brain will increase and the number
of faster waves will decrease (*see* page
29). Like the previous sleep stages, it is
a NREM phase of sleep. These stages
typically start 35–45 minutes after
falling asleep and are extremely
rejuvenating for the body.

Stages three and four of sleep are often
the most challenging to wake up from.
Slow-wave sleep is the deepest sleep
that your body enters throughout the
night, so if you are woken up during
this phase, you will most likely be really
groggy and disoriented. During these
stages, your breathing becomes deeper,
your blood pressure drops, there is no
eye movement and your body becomes
immobile. However, even though there
is no muscle movement, your muscles
still have the ability to function. (These
are the stages when children sometimes
experience nightmares, bedwetting
and sleepwalking.)

STAGE FIVE

ALSO KNOWN AS REM

REM sleep
✱ *When most dreams occur*

Stage five makes up to 25 per cent of your sleeping time. It first occurs about 90 minutes after falling asleep and recurs about every 90 minutes. The first REM sleep stage lasts around 10 minutes, but it gets longer as you continue in the sleep cycle. During REM sleep, the eyes dart back and forth and your body becomes immobile and relaxed as the muscles are turned off. It is when your brain is active and dreams occur.

Stage five is the only stage of REM and is unlike any other sleep phase because the brain is bursting with activity. Most adults spend about 20 per cent of sleep in REM, while infants spend almost 50 per cent. Research shows that as we age

we spend less time in REM sleep. Varying theories point to changes of sleeping patterns due to the ageing process, physical illness and disease, medications, insomnia, snoring, restless leg syndrome and menopause.

Most dreaming takes place in stage five as a result of heightened, desynchronized brain waves that are almost similar to being awake. This stage of sleep will revitalize your brain and body, supporting sharp and alert daytime function. You will typically spend up to 90 minutes during your sleep dreaming.

THE CYCLE REPEATS

After REM sleep, you will return to stage one of light sleep and begin a new cycle. As the time spent asleep in the sleep cycle progresses, you will spend increasingly more time in REM sleep and correspondingly less time in deep sleep.

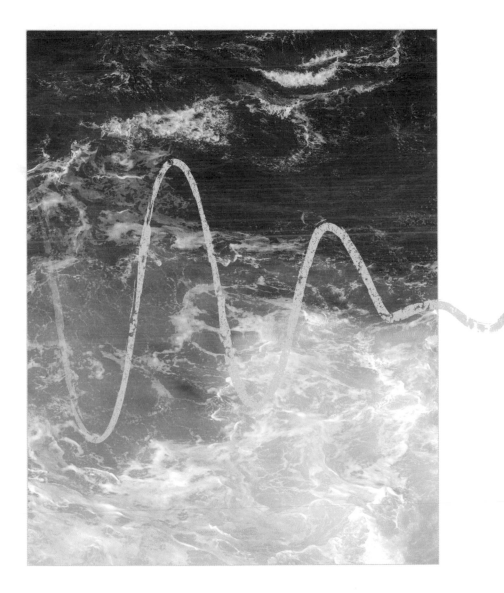

Brain waves

Your brain is a remarkable machine. It contains billions of neurons (nerve cells) and is able to process thoughts at thousands of miles per second. Using electricity, these neurons talk to each other to help your brain function. All of this communication produces enough electrical activity that it can be observed using specific scientific equipment such as an electroencephalograph (EEG) machine.

Brain-wave patterns and hertz scale

This accumulation of electrical activity is known as neural oscillation. It is also referred to as a brain-wave pattern because the EEG reading resembles a wave. This is because the neurons have a burst (or pulse) of firings, are silent and then have a burst of firings again in a repeating cycle. Brain waves are important because they are indicators of what is occurring inside the brain. There are specific patterns and these can signify which particular state of being you are in.

Each different brain-wave pattern has a range of frequency based on the hertz scale. The frequency is measured in pulses per second. A measurement of 15 hertz (Hz), for example, means there are 15 pulses (bursts of firings) per second. Brain waves play an important role in the function of sleep and dreaming. During your sleep cycle, your brain waves fluctuate between different brain-wave states, thus affecting whether or not you are in light sleep or deep sleep. Let's get to know the brain waves.

TYPES OF BRAIN WAVES

GAMMA

Gamma waves are known for conscious attention, inspiration and higher learning. They are often found to be present during certain Buddhist meditations. Gamma waves exist at 30–100+ Hz.

BETA

Beta waves are emitted when you are consciously alert and awake. This is your primary waking frequency and they are responsible for concentration and cognition. Beta waves have a range of 12–30 Hz. They have the highest frequency and lowest amplitude when compared to other waves. These patterns also show a lot of variability.

ALPHA

Alpha waves have a deeper wave pattern that are present during states of physical and mental relaxation. You can still be aware of everything around you, but you are feeling creative and deeply relaxed. These have a range of 8–12 Hz.

THETA

Theta waves occur during stages one and two in the sleep cycle and are slower in frequency and greater in amplitude than alpha waves. Theta waves have a range of 4–8 Hz. As you move from stage one to stage two in the sleep cycle, theta-wave activity continues; every few minutes, sleep spindles (sudden increases in wave *frequency*) and K-complexes (sudden increases in wave *amplitude*) occur. These waves are often also associated with daydreaming or feeling sleepy. They are associated with meditation, intuition and memory. They are also strongly associated with creative states.

DELTA

Delta waves occur during stages three and four sleep and are the slowest waves with the highest amplitude. Delta sleep is the deepest sleep. The waves have a range of 0.1–4 Hz and represent the lowest amount of activity possible. Delta waves typically occur only during deep sleep, and they can also trigger growth and body healing.

PART 2

Sleep Hygiene

What is sleep hygiene?

On hearing the word "hygiene", some people may feel a squeamish aversion. It is one of those tactile words that can put us off or make us feel slightly paranoid about our bodily maintenance. However, the same should not be true for the term "sleep hygiene".

The idea of sleep hygiene was first developed in 1939 by the physiologist and sleep researcher Nathaniel Kleitman, although similar concepts were explored 75 years earlier by scientist and professor Paolo Mantegazza in his works published in 1864. Many years later, in 1977, psychologist Peter Hauri resurrected the concept of sleep hygiene in his published writings, and the ideas have continued to evolve. A lot of research has gone into creating a template of guidelines to help promote good sleep, and there is plenty of evidence to suggest that these tips can provide long-standing solutions for people with sleep difficulties.

So what is sleep hygiene and what does hygiene have to do with sleeping?

Sleep hygiene is a combination of behavioural tasks and environmental improvement factors that help aid a better quality of sleep.

Lifestyle factors are an important element when cultivating your conscious dreaming practice. Being mindful of your habits during the day, your sleeping environment and making necessary healthy changes can vastly improve both your sleep and your dreaming time.

Sleep schedule

An important aspect of implementing good sleep hygiene is knowing how much sleep you need. Throughout our lives, our sleep needs will change. Infants, children and adolescents need far more sleep than adults, and according to the National Sleep Foundation, adults typically require between 7 and 9 hours of sleep at a time. For adults getting less sleep than this, sleep deprivation is associated with a variety of physical and mental-health deficits.

How much sleep do you need?

If you feel unrested after sleeping and you decide to take on the challenge of improving your sleep schedule, it is useful to know how much sleep is right for you. You may need more or less sleep than the recommended amount. A good way to start is to make sure you allow enough time to get to bed and sleep for at least 7 hours. If you do this for a week and you still wake up feeling unrested, then gradually increase your sleeping time. However, if you find that you wake up energized and rested after only 6½ hours sleep, you have no need to worry. The key here is not that you get the "official" amount of sleep but that you feel well rested.

Each individual is different in this respect and it will take some conscious awareness and experimenting with your sleep schedule to find your optimum number of hours. There is one caveat regarding a sleep schedule: if you are getting less than 6 hours or more than 9 hours and still do not feel rested, you may have a sleeping disorder. You should make an appointment with your doctor to investigate this possibility.

TIPS FOR A SUCCESSFUL SLEEP SCHEDULE

* Go to bed at the same time every day.
* Get up at the same time every day.
* Try to maintain your sleep schedule, say, on days off work to avoid repercussions when returning.
* Get 7–9 hours of sleep each day.
* Avoid bedtime procrastination.
* Follow a bedtime routine.
* Set an alarm for waking up.

Body

Understand your body clock! Also known as the circadian rhythm, your body clock is an internal cycle that tells you when to sleep, rise and eat, and it regulates a number of physiological processes.

This innate body clock is affected by environmental cues such as sunlight and temperature. Circadian rhythms can influence sleep-wake cycles, your body temperature, eating habits and digestion, and hormone release. Exercise is also an important aspect in either facilitating or inhibiting your quality of sleep. Individuals who exercise will usually experience better-quality sleep than those who do not.

Affects of light
Your sleep-wake cycle is closely connected to your circadian rhythms. Your brain relies on sunshine during the day to recognize it's time to be awake and alert. The more natural light you receive, the more your body stays in tune to the regular day-night rhythms. The brain associates the darkness that comes in the evening with falling asleep, so that's why it's important to limit your exposure to bright light from electronics before going to bed.

HOW TO HELP
YOUR BODY CLOCK

✳ Get regular exercise of up to 20 minutes every day, preferably in the morning. Avoid any strenuous exercise within 6 hours of your bedtime.

✳ Get regular exposure to sunshine or bright lights, especially in the morning.

✳ Limit your daytime naps. They can inhibit your ability to fall asleep at night.

✳ If you do nap, limit them to short power naps of less than 30 minutes.

✳ If you do not sleep well, avoid changing your routine the next day. In particular, avoid increasing your caffeine intake, as this will most likely just keep you up again.

Diet and substances

Effectively, if you want to sleep better, it helps to put only good things in your body. A nutritious diet and healthy lifestyle habits help to support higher-quality sleep and therefore connect you more to your dreaming time.

There are a number of foods and substances that are known to disturb the quality of sleep. Stimulants – such as caffeine found in coffee, fizzy drinks and chocolate – and an upset stomach can leave a sleeper tossing and turning all night and waking up groggy and unrested. Alcohol and prescribed (as well as recreational) drugs can also impact sleep.

Staying hydrated is key to good health, but watch your water intake before going to bed, too. Use the toilet one last time before bed to avoid being woken by a full bladder.

IN THE HOURS LEADING UP TO BEDTIME

✳ Avoid alcohol. While alcohol can make you drowsy and initially induce sleep, it disrupts sleep in the latter part of the sleep cycle, preventing you getting essential amounts of REM and deep sleep.

✳ Avoid sleeping pills, or use them cautiously. Most doctors do not prescribe sleeping pills for periods of more than 3 weeks. Do not drink alcohol while taking sleeping pills.

✳ Avoid large meals and a full stomach – you will be more likely to have nightmares, and the effort required to digest a big meal can impede sleep.

✳ Avoid food that can be disruptive such as heavy, rich foods and fatty, fried or spicy dishes.

✳ Avoid being too hungry at bedtime – it can cause insomnia.

✳ Avoid sugar and fizzy drinks.

✳ Avoid nicotine.

✳ Avoid caffeine.

Mind

Although you need to be conscious of your body as you begin to implement a healthy sleep hygiene schedule, you also need to take care of your mind. Your cognitive activity around bedtime can greatly affect your ability to have a restful sleep, therefore engaging in relaxing activities before sleep is highly recommended. The following advice can help prepare your mind for sleeping.

Avoid electronics

Disconnect from all your electronics at least an hour before bed – and do not take them to bed with you. The noisy chatter of social media, television advertisements and news channels is the last thing you want to take with you to bed, and being actively involved in checking an email or playing a game can keep your brain going. Additionally, the blue light emitted by television, computer, laptop and smartphone screens can deceive your brain into believing it is time to be awake. Blue light is the strongest wavelength of light that your brain perceives as sunlight.

Do not worry

Avoid taking your worries to bed with you. Designate an earlier time in your day to write down your tasks, worries, problems and to-do lists. Positive sleep hygiene involves minimizing time spent thinking about worries or anything emotionally upsetting shortly before bedtime. Instead, focus on your conscious dreaming practice at bedtime (*see* page 59 on Mindful intent).

Do not get worked up

Avoid emotional drama or arguments before bed. Anything that winds you up, triggers your emotions and gets your mind spinning will interrupt your sleep.

Do not force it

Avoid commanding yourself to go to sleep. Trying too hard to control your sleep will make you more tense and more awake. Stay calm when you cannot sleep. Whatever you do, however, do not turn on your electronics!

Do not be a timekeeper

Avoid constantly looking at your watch, phone or alarm clock to check the time. This is a common cause of insomnia.

Do relax

Practise relaxing rituals prior to bedtime (*see* page 84 on Dream plants and herbs and page 59 on Mindful intent).

Environment

Your bed and bedroom are fundamentally important for both good sleep hygiene and your conscious dreaming practice. The environment of a room affects both the psychological and physical components of sleep and dreaming. You should be seeing your bed and bedroom as a sacred space for sleep and dreaming time, or as a specially equipped spaceship that flies you off to dreamland every night. Here are some suggestions to help you make your room the optimum place for positive sleep and dream incubation.

Remove all electronics

Dedicate your bed to sleep and sex, and nothing else! Having a dedicated place for sleep is psychologically important. Many people have televisions, laptops and electronic tablets in their bedrooms. Get all of them out of there! Make your bed a sacred space so you will not be tempted to watch Netflix or work on your laptop, which impacts on your mind and sleep (*see* page 38). Leave all your electronics in another room, with the exception of your smartphone but only if you need to keep this handy for your dream journaling (*see* page 73),

Eliminate a visible bedroom clock to prevent focusing on time passing when trying to fall asleep. Get strict with yourself. You will see the big difference it makes to the quality of your sleep and in creating a deeper connection to your dreams. Be disciplined enough to implement this and make new associations when it comes to how you should use your bed.

Quiet room

Your bedroom should be as quiet as possible. Of course, for many of us, this is impossible. Living in big cities, on high-traffic roads or next to a fire station will not be helpful. If this is your situation, investing in earplugs or playing white noise in your room could help block out city noises. In this case, you can use an electronic device, ideally placed a good distance away from your head, to play white noise or ambient sounds such as a trickling stream as you sleep.

If you live in a noisy neighbourhood or have noisy neighbours, you could invest in soundproofing, place furniture strategically against shared walls to absorb sound or use thick curtains to help absorb sound coming in from the windows via the street. Another alternative is to consider moving! As drastic as this sounds, if noise is short-changing you of sleep night after night, it is effectively lessening your quality of life and should be taken seriously.

Temperature and air quality

The best temperature for sleep is around 18.5°C (65°F). Maintaining a consistently cool temperature helps your body thermoregulate during sleep. Having the right humidity in your bedroom is helpful, too. Central heating can make the air in some bedrooms too dry in the winter, but other homes struggle with the air being too damp. Air pollution can also affect air quality, whether from busy traffic, wood-burning stoves, open fires or other sources. You may find that fans, humidifiers, dehumidifiers, air purifiers or other devices can make the temperature and air quality of your room more desirable.

Lighting

Keeping your bedroom dark also keeps it cool by blocking out heat from sunlight in the morning. Some of us live in cooler, darker climates, so this won't be an issue. However, most importantly, the darkness convinces your brain that it's night-time, so if you live in a light-polluted city, wake up too early at sunrise, or work at night and sleep during the day, you might want to invest in either blackout curtains or an eye mask to help you sleep.

Night lights might be suitable for some people, but light-sensitive people can find them disruptive. Avoid turning on the main, full light if you need to get up and use the toilet during the night. Even a quick, small blast of full-spectrum light in the dead of night can make it more challenging to get back to sleep.

Room colour

The colour of the walls of your room can affect your mood. Choose colours that you find calm and soothing. These might be neutral, light shades of blue, whites or yellows. Search for what feels right for you and consider a fresh coat of paint in your bedroom.

Your bed and bedding

The place where you lay your head down to sleep and dream should be taken seriously! One-third of your life is spent asleep. I would say that's enough time to warrant a good investment for an ideal bed.

Selecting the appropriate mattress, pillows and bedclothes can affect your sleep enormously. Of course, this will differ from person to person. One individual may prefer a firm mattress whereas another prefers soft. Make a conscious effort to think about what works for you and what your ideal bed would be. Do you need plenty of room to stretch out? Do you have specific pillow requirements? Do you get too hot with heavy bedclothes? Spend some time reflecting on your dream bed and write down your requirements. You don't need to break the bank to achieve your ideal bed, but with some reflection, research and planning you can most likely find one that suits your needs both physically and financially.

As well as investing in a good mattress and pillows, choose comfortable bedding. Look for 100 per cent cotton sheets, which breathe better as you sleep. Synthetic materials can become too hot and scratchy and might disrupt your sleep. Consider the colour theme of your bedding. Soothing colours help promote a soothing mind. You might want to avoid garish and over-stimulating colours and patterns.

Declutter

Spring-clean your room and remove the stagnant and stale energy of unnecessary clutter. If you are finding it challenging to get rid of old things or move them from your room into another one, just ask yourself the question: does having this in here help promote my sleep or inspire my dreams? Remove clutter and items that remind you of work from your room as well as visible objects of clutter such as clothes, boxes and books.

If you live somewhere tiny and space is a challenge, try setting up the area around your actual bed to be as decluttered as possible. Perhaps you can use curtains or folding screens to hide the bulk of the clutter in a section of the room.

Cleanliness

Regular cleaning is important to keep your bedroom fresh. This not only includes cleaning the bedroom itself but also your mattress and bedclothes. Ideally, your mattress should be cleaned at the turn of every season, or at least once a year. Strip your mattress of all bedding and use a vacuum cleaner to clean its surface and seams. Flip it over to vacuum its underside as well. Always use a mattress protector to create a layer between you, your bedsheets and the mattress.

Bedding and pillowcases should be washed on a weekly basis to remove the build-up of dirt, sweat, hair, body fluids, bacteria and dead skin that is left behind as you sleep. It will also help ensure that your bedding smells fresh and pleasant, which promotes comfort during sleeping time.

Duvets, comforters and pillows should, ideally, be washed every few months to combat dust mites, skin scales and fungus. The same goes for your nightclothes. Ideally, they should be washed every two wears or at least once a week. I'm sure that we can all agree that sliding into fresh, clean bed linen and nightclothes is a wonderful, cosy and relaxing sensation.

Aroma

Along with the cleanliness of your bedroom comes the sense of smell. Fresh, clean fragrances aid relaxation and promote pleasant moods. If your bedroom is smelling stale, of stinky laundry and bedding, leftover food, cigarette smoke or body odour, it will not exactly feel like a place where you want to spend time, let alone sleep in! Make sure you air out your bedroom regularly by opening the window. Good times to do this are just before bed and right when you wake up. There are also a variety of essential oils that you can use in your bedroom to help introduce a pleasant aroma and mood.

Plants

Once you've removed all electronics and clutter from your room, you can replace it all with some living energy in the form of plants. As well as aesthetically improving the look of your home, plants can bring life and vitality to your bedroom and provide relaxing and purifying benefits that can positively improve the quality of your sleep. Studies show that being immersed in nature assists in the feeling of wellbeing and relaxation. I'm sure that all of us can agree that we feel relaxed and happy when we are walking in a forest or sitting quietly in a field of flowers.

According to the US NASA Clean Air Study, there are a variety of plants that you can add to your home to help clean the air. So as well as providing relaxing and calming effects in your sleeping environment, they can also help you to breathe fresher air as you sleep.

I have listed 12 of my favourite air-cleaning plants, along with some care instructions, on the following pages.

Plants for improving air quality and promoting healthy sleep

MOTHER-IN-LAW'S TONGUE/ SNAKE PLANT

The great thing about mother-in-law's tongue, apart from looking really alien and cool, is that it emits oxygen at night while simultaneously taking in carbon dioxide. It also works hard to remove harmful household toxins from the air such as formaldehyde, benzene, xylene, toluene and trichloroethylene. This all results in better-quality air in your bedroom and a better sleep. It is an amazingly low-maintenance plant, so I highly recommend it for those who are novice houseplant owners.

Plant care

* Loves indirect sunlight.
* Allow the soil to dry between waterings.
* Avoid overwatering.
* Avoid getting the leaves wet and keep them well dusted.

SPIDER PLANT

You cannot have a mother-in-law's tongue without adding a spider plant to the mix! The spider plant is also in the top list of air-purifying plants. According to the US NASA Clean Air Study, the spider plant can eliminate 90 per cent of the potentially carcinogenic chemical formaldehyde from the air. Just like the mother-in-law's tongue, it is also low maintenance, making it an ideal plant for beginners.

Plant care

* Loves indirect sunlight.
* Allow the soil to dry between waterings.
* Avoid overwatering.
* Avoid getting the leaves wet and keep them well dusted.

PEACE LILY

One of my favourite bedroom plants is the peace lily. Not only is it gorgeous and expressive, it is also an amazing air cleaner. Much like the mother-in-law's tongue, it helps to filter out household toxins from the air in your home. Also, the moisture given off by this lovely plant can boost the humidity in the room by up to 5 per cent. This, in return, can help relieve any dry throats or noses that keep you up all night.

Plant care

* Give it evenly moist, well-drained soil.
* If the leaves wilt every 2–3 days, repot into a bigger pot or water more often.
* Loves indirect light.
* Feed with a fertilizer.

ALOE VERA

I can't say enough about this healing little plant! Aloe vera will be a brilliant addition to your household, improving your sleep environment and wellbeing in general. Not only does it oxygenate your room and improve the air quality, it also embodies some medicinal qualities. You can use the gel of the aloe vera plant as a topical treatment for insect bites, dry skin, burns, minor cuts and more. It's no wonder the Native Americans refer to it as "the wand of heaven" and the ancient Egyptians called it "the plant of immortality".

Plant care

* Only water when the soil is completely dry.
* Keep in a dry environment.
* Add drainage holes to the pot.
* Loves the sun, so keep near a window.

GARDENIA

One of the most exquisite flowering houseplants, the gardenia is also often used as an ornamental shrub. Studies indicate that crocetin, the active carotenoid compound of gardenia, can significantly improve the quality of sleep. The gardenia has one of the most pleasant aromas of any flower that you can grow. It is similar to jasmine in both appearance and scent, along with its effect on you as a person.

Simply smelling the flowers will sedate you, making it easy for you to get to sleep. Some people even use gardenias and jasmine in place of sleeping pills as an eco-friendly and natural way to deal with their sleep issues.

Plant care

* Loves the sun, so place it in front of a window.
* Keep the soil moist but well drained.
* Feed with a plant fertilizer.

IVY

Ivy is a great option if you're looking to add a dash of greenery to your bedroom. Not only is it gorgeous to look at – there's your pretty corner accent – it also helps purify the air inside your house. The NASA Clean Air Study found that ivy can reduce the amount of mold spores in your home environment. So keeping an ivy plant in the bedroom or elsewhere can help people with mold allergies who experience mild to severe symptoms.

However, ivy is also a poisonous plant, so take care to keep the plant out of the reach of children and pets who may be attracted to the leaves and berries. The sap from the plant can also cause skin reactions in some people.

Plant care

* Keep in a shady spot with indirect sunlight.
* Prune regularly.
* Keep away from draughty areas.
* Water when the soil is dry to touch.

ARECA PALM/BAMBOO PALM

Transform your bedroom into a tropical and exotic environment. The areca palm will not only make you feel like you are on holiday, but it will improve the quality of the air while you sleep. This is another NASA-certified plant that helps purify the air by removing toxins.

Plant care

* Can grow in low-lit areas, but prefers indirect bright light.
* Whenever the soil feels dry, water it evenly so all of the soil is moist.
* Avoid overwatering.

GERBERA

Add some colour to your room with this bright and cheerful flowering plant. The daisy-like flowers come in an array of joyful colours, including yellow, pink, orange, purple and white. Not only does a gerbera look happy, but it will also help you feel happy. It releases oxygen at night, which can help promote a happy and healthy sleep.

Plant care

* Loves the sun.
* Loves sandy soils.
* Water regularly, except when flowering.
* Can require special attention as it is prone to fungal diseases.

DEVIL'S IVY/GOLDEN POTHOS

Here is another champion of air purification! And the cascading vines of this exotic-looking plant can make your bedroom feel like the Hanging Gardens of Babylon. If you live in a city, consider placing it near your bedroom window to detoxify any air that may be coming in. This plant requires little nurturing and needs low levels of sunlight, so is perfect for those with a busy schedule.

Plant care

* Prefers indirect sunlight.
* Make sure that the soil is completely dry before watering to avoid root rot.
* The leaves are toxic, so keep out of the reach of pets and children.

LAVENDER

The smell of lavender is well recognized as a great aid for relaxation. Lavender has been proven to lower heart rates, blood pressure and stress levels, which is why it's perfect for the bedroom. A study by the Miami Miller School of Medicine even showed that the scent of lavender in bath oil calms babies and sends them into a deeper sleep, while also reducing stress in the mother.

Plant care

* ✳ Loves a sunny windowsill.
* ✳ Water sparingly when the soil is dry to the touch.
* ✳ Avoid overwatering – the roots are prone to rot from excess water.

HOUSEPLANT TIPS

✳ If you have pets or children, always make sure the plants are non-toxic!

✳ Wipe off dust build-up from the leaves of your plants. This will help them to properly filter air.

JASMINE

The gentle and soothing effects of jasmine make it an ideal bedroom plant but it does require some extra care. The flowers of this lovely vine are very pretty and exude a relaxing, sweet scent. Jasmine is often used in aromatherapy for its calming effects. Studies show that the scent of jasmine can reduce anxiety levels, leading to a better quality of sleep.

Plant care

* Sun lover in spring and summer but prefers indirect sunlight in winter.
* Grow in a hanging basket or pot.
* Keep the soil moist and well drained during summer, allowing it to dry between waterings, but water less during winter and spring.
* Prune thoroughly in spring.

VALERIAN

A perennial flowering houseplant, valerian has beautiful, scented flowers. It is said that the Roman philosopher Galen prescribed valerian as a cure for insomnia. Recent findings back Galen's theory; it has been proven that inhaling the scent of valerian can increase the duration of quality sleep. Currently, it is used as a primary ingredient in products that have sedative effects.

Plant care

* Loves a windowsill or well-lit room.
* Provide at least 6 hours of direct sunlight each day.
* Water every 2 days.

PART 3

The Foundations of a Conscious Dreaming Practice

Getting started

Now that you know how your sleep cycle works, you will be better prepared for embracing some of the foundations of my conscious dreaming practice.

The foundations that I outline in this section are a series of new positive, inspiring, creative, mindful, healthy and pragmatic "habits" that you can implement into your daily life. These new routines are all centred around your sleep, dreaming time, lifestyle habits, environment, daily and nightly rituals, and your mindful outlook. They will not only benefit your sleep and dreams but will also bring positive and healthy changes to your mind, body and spirit.

Mindful intent

An important aspect of your conscious dreaming practice is your daily mindset. Mindful intent is the psychological process of drawing attention to your present mental state and, through your will, of deciding how to carry out an action either in that moment or as a goal for the future.

The way in which you navigate and manage your day-to-day thoughts, perception and awareness has a direct effect not only on your waking life but also on your dreaming. If you become more present, mindful and conscious of your thoughts, behaviours and unconscious emotional triggers, then you will be more able to carry them through into your dreaming time.

Being aware of your dreams

As a conscious dreamer, the goal is to be able to evolve to the point where you are always, to varying degrees, conscious and aware within your dreams. Of course, this awareness will naturally be sharper at times than others, much like when we are awake. You will have moments in your waking life when you are present, focused, really observing and taking in the moment. And then you will have times when you are daydreaming, distracted by thoughts or mentally sleepwalking throughout your day.

For many oneironauts, or dream travellers, the pinnacle achievement of being a conscious dreamer would be to experience a lucid dream, one in which you are fully present and that you can control. But your consciousness and awareness can also be silently observing in all of your other genres of dreams as well. You might not necessarily be able to control these particular dreams, but you can observe, learn and watch them unfold into meaning.

On the following pages are tips to help you implement mindful intent throughout your day and train both your waking and dreaming mind to become more aware, observant and present.

Embracing self-awareness

For the most part, people seem to journey through their day-to-day lives without really noticing or even questioning the world around them. They walk through their daily lives rarely pausing to contemplate the clouds moving across the sky or the wind rustling through the leaves of the trees. They take these things for granted and just never really observe them or even question them. The same can be said of the dreamworld, too. It is easy to shrug off your dreams and not engage with them.

A good start to becoming more self-aware is to decide to contemplate, question and observe your reality on a regular basis. You will find that this actually increases your self-awareness in your day-to-day life and you will become more present and in the moment. You will eventually find that this becomes your default setting of perception and consciousness in both your waking life and your dreams.

There is no quick-fix solution to having consistent self-awareness. As with all practices, the more you practise self-awareness, the better you will become in achieving it. The following steps will help you to improve your self-awareness.

OBSERVE

At times when you are alone – it could be when sitting in a park or commuting on a train – challenge yourself to really observe your surroundings. Perhaps you are watching a dog owner play fetch with his dog or you are simply watching green fields pass by on a train journey. Whatever your environment, let your awareness hone in and focus on it. You do not need to think too much about it. Just observe, as you would a film.

STUDY

As you are watching a scene unfold, choose something in your environment to study. I mean REALLY study. It could be a beautiful flower that is in the grass in the park you are sitting in, or it could be the red apple you just bought for your train commute. Challenge yourself to study it in detail: the colours, the shape, the texture.

ANALYSE

As you are studying your chosen object, begin to analyse it. REALLY analyse it. Was there something that you did not notice before when you were merely studying this object? Was there something that you missed? Look at how it is structured and put together.

QUESTION

Begin to question the object. What is this flower for? How did it get here? Is it moving in the wind or is the wind moving it?

EXPLORE

Let your mind move in and out of the questioning and observing mode. You will notice that something interesting happens. You begin to start to question your own reality! This can be a fascinating head zone for some or trippy for others. This zone is similar to various exploratory states we have as children. It can be playful and joyful and is a great practice for when you begin to explore in lucid dreams.

Reality checks

Now that you know the steps to embracing self-awareness, it will be easier for you to create a mental habit of reality checking.

The key element to lucidity in a dream is being able to notice the difference between a dream and waking reality.

When we dream, we are unconscious and unaware and accept it as "reality". But when we wake up, we have our "Ah ha!" moment of, "It was only a dream!" By implementing reality checks in your daily life, you will soon find that it carries through into your dreams and eventually you will have your "Ah ha!" moment within the dream itself.

HOW TO PERFORM A REALITY CHECK

Fundamental questions are asked during a reality check such as; "Is this reality or a dream?" and "Am I awake right now or am I dreaming?" A reality check involves applying this line of questioning along with a paradoxical predetermined action. Many dreamers choose to use their hands (because they are always with them), and the steps here are based on using your hands.

* Hold out your hands.

* Really study them.

* Engage in your line of questioning: "Is this reality or a dream?" "Am I awake right now or am I dreaming?"

* Try to push two fingers from your right hand through the palm of your left hand.

* Will your fingers to pass through the palm of your hand.

* Repeat your line of questioning: "Is this reality or a dream?" "Am I awake right now or am I dreaming?

Of course, in waking life, the physics of this reality check experiment would make it impossible for your fingers to pass through the palm of your hand. But in a dream it's an entirely different experience. When you do find yourself looking at your hands in your dream, your mind will be trained for a reality check, and when you attempt to push your fingers through the palm of your opposite hand, they will most likely pass right through! This is a great opportunity to bridge into a Lucid dream (see page 132).

Conscious affirmations

Another way to cultivate your mindful intent is through conscious affirmations. A good time to do this is before you go to sleep. As you lay your head down on the pillow, run through a few conscious affirmations in your mind. Some examples are:

* I will have a lucid dream tonight.

* I will remember my dreams tonight

Really feel your affirmations and stay focused on them. Repeat the affirmations until you feel drowsy.

Set your intent

If you are preparing a dream herb tea before bed, you can set your intent at this time. Alternatively, you can set it after your conscious affirmations. Your intent is your goal for your dreams. Some examples are:

* I will find my hands in my dreams tonight.

* I will find a door in my dreams tonight.

* I will meet a dream character and they will teach me something new.

* I will work through my emotional challenges in my dreams tonight.

Visualize your intent

As you slip into the hypnagogic state (*see* page 22), you can start to actively visualize your intent in your mind's eye. Some examples are:

* Visualize your hands held open in front of you.

* Visualize a door and opening that door, and then let the scene unfold.

* Visualize a dream character.

* Visualize yourself overcoming your emotional challenges.

Reread your dream journal

Rereading and reflecting upon old dreams will help you to stay connected to them. Reading and sharing your dreams with others can also help to trigger new dreams, or give you inspiration to progress some existing dreams. If a particular dream inspired you in the past, you can set your intent before you fall asleep to re-enter that dream to see how it evolves. This is known as progressive dreaming.

Dream shrine

Another way to keep engaged with your mindful intent is to create a dream shrine. A dream shrine is a designated place in your room where you keep all of your dreaming tools, inspirations and goals. It can be the place that you touch base with at bedtime when you set your intents, as well as in the mornings when you wake up and record your dreams.

HOW TO CREATE YOUR OWN DREAM SHRINE

You can get as creative or inspired with your dream shrine as you want to be. It can be a motivating project that helps you get started with your conscious dreaming practice. Find a surface area in your room that you can dedicate to your dream shrine. Gather together all the objects and tools that you use or that inspire you for sleep or dreaming. Some examples are:

* Dream journal

* Dream herbs and plants

* Dreaming stones or crystals

* Images of personal dream symbols

* Images of your intents or goals

* Objects that represent your personal mythology

* Candles

* Essential oils for sleep and dreaming

* Sage, palo santo wood (an aromatic incense wood from South America) or incense

* Sketches, drawings or artwork of your dreams

Dream journaling

One fundamental key to a conscious dreaming practice is the journaling or recording of your dreams. You can journal your dreams by writing them down, or you can film or record yourself retelling your dream experience. Journaling your dreams will enable you to improve your dream memory recall, help trigger more dreams, act as markers along your spiritual/creative path, provide insight into your inner world and also serve as proof of any Precognitive dreams (*see* page 140) you may experience.

A record for interpreting your dreams

Dream journaling will also greatly assist you in delving deep into the meanings of dream symbols and recurrent patterns or themes. Your dreams are continuously communicating with you and are innately linked to an effective comprehension of the emotions and wellbeing of your waking life.

Recording your dreams can help prompt you to look at important aspects within the dream that needs interpretation. It can serve as markers to point you toward an aspect of your life that may need some extra attention. Effectively, a dream journal is like the writings of your unconscious world and your soul. It serves as a brilliant tool as you become consciously aware of, and subsequently begin to work in partnership with, this deeper aspect of yourself.

Once you begin journaling, you will also start to notice the unique language of dreams: surreal, poetic, symbolic,

mystical, playful, absurd and sometimes eery. You may find that some of your dreams appear to read from the pages of a David Lynch film, whereas others seem to play out like a Monty Python skit. Dreams, if taken literally, can be mind-boggling and mysterious, so practising dream journaling can greatly help to accurately decode and demystify them. No matter how it all unfolds in your writings, the important aspect is to let the dream flow out in its entirety onto the pages of your diary in articulated detail.

One thing to note: recording your dreams requires some self-discipline, but once you incorporate it into your morning routine as a ritual practice, it will most likely become a long-term habit. This newly formed habit will not only be a practical one but also bring into your daily life a new richness of personal reflection, creativity, inner connection, spiritual purpose, guidance and maybe even a bit of entertainment.

Creativity and problem-solving

One of the inspiring repercussions of recording your dreams is that they can act as a muse for creativity. They can even help with scientific and mathematical problem-solving or troubleshooting. There are countless examples of artist, musicians, scientists and mathematicians who have made creative and innovative breakthroughs with the help of their dreams.

Whether you are a musician, an artist, a biologist, a product designer or a software engineer, you can look to your dreams as a sounding board or sketchbook for your unfolding ideas. Dream journaling can help you to access some of the inspired ideas that come through in dreams and then develop them further.

KEWPIE DOLLS

In the early 1900s American artist Rose O'Neill was inspired by dreams of chubby, cherubic characters performing acrobatic pranks at the end of her bed. Both obsessed and inspired by her dream, O'Neill evolved the idea and in 1909 the "Kewpies" made their debut as a comic strip. Eventually, this led to the production of dolls and other merchandise and amassed O'Neill a fortune.

GOOGLE

In the 1990s, computer scientist Larry Page had a dream about downloading the entire web. In the dream, he examined the links between pages and as a result saw the world's information in a completely different way. Upon waking, in the middle of the night, he wrote all the details of the dream down and eventually worked out the basis for an algorithm. This would become the search engine Google, and now a multinational technology company worth billions.

FRANKENSTEIN

In 1816, writer Mary Shelley had a nightmare of a reconstructed corpse coming to life with the aid of a man with a powerful engine. This nightmare would become the inspiration of her gothic horror classic *Frankenstein*.

DISCOVERY
OF A MOLECULE

One of the most famous examples of ideas forming from dreams is the discovery of benzene by German chemist August Kekulé. He said that he had discovered the ring shape of the benzene molecule after having a dream of a snake seizing its own tail, like the ancient symbol known as the Ouroboros. *Ouroboros* is Greek for "tail-devourer", and the symbol depicts a serpent forming a circle as it perpetually swallows its own tail and is reborn.

CHOOSING A DREAM JOURNAL

Here are some things to consider when deciding on a method for recording your dreams. You can also use a combination of these methods if you wish.

Writing a journal

If you decide to keep a written dream journal, think carefully about how you will use it. Here are several points to consider when deciding on a suitable journal that will be right for you.

THE JOURNAL'S SIZE

You might want a size that is portable so you can carry it around in your bag, giving you access to it when you want to reflect on your dreams. A smaller journal can be particularly useful if you travel a lot (*see* page 74). Or you may prefer a larger-size journal that gives you space to sketch your dreams *and* write down your interpretations of them.

THE COVER

You could purchase a ready-made dream journal or get creative and make your own. Over the years, I have always found it fun to have a variety of different-looking journals. Drawing or making collages on the covers gives a specific personality to the journal you are using, plus it can make it easier to access certain dream records from over the years based on the uniqueness of the journal cover.

THE PAGES INSIDE

Think about the organizational aspect of your dream record-keeping and what suits you best. Consider the number of pages in the journal. It's possible you would like to record your dreams for an entire year and so purchase a yearly dream journal. Or perhaps it makes more sense to you to record your dreams on a monthly basis.

You might find a journal that enables you to hold scraps of paper will be useful, too. If you remember dreams throughout the day and jot them down on loose paper, you can add these to your journal later.

Alternatively, a journal in a binder with loose pages will allow you to add pages or move them around. This might be handy if you want to type out your dreams and then print them out. It is also useful if you want to categorize your dreams into various themed sections, such as recurring dreams or precognitive dreams.

WRITING TOOLS

If you go the traditional route and decide to keep a dream journal at your bedside, remember to keep a pen alongside it! Many dreamers have experienced waking up to a remarkable dream, grabbed their journals off the bedside table to record the "fresh off the press" dream and...no pen! So save yourself a lot of fumbling around in the morning and make sure your trusty pen is there with your journal.

It is also helpful to have some kind of light source by your bedside for those moments when you wake up in the dead of night with an inspired dream to write down. If a bedside lamp is unavailable to you, perhaps a small torch or flashlight will do.

Audio recording

If you find that writing in a journal the old-fashioned way is not for you, consider recording yourself recounting your dream. There are a variety of electronic devices out there that can do the job of audio recording, but probably the most universal and easily accessible one is on your smartphone. Most smartphones come with a recording feature or have the ability to install a voice recorder app.

Video recording

If you are not camera-shy and don't mind filming yourself first thing in the morning, or in the middle of the night after an epic lucid dream, you might prefer to film yourself recounting your experience. Again, most smartphones have video-recording features and you can use these as your tool. The key is to have these tools charged up and easy to access when you wake from sleep and are ready to record your dream.

THE FOUNDATIONS OF A CONSCIOUS DREAMING PRACTICE

PREPARING TO JOURNAL

Once you have decided on your preferred journaling method and acquired the tools you will need, you will want to keep these next to or close to your bed. One way of ensuring that all of your dream-recording tools are in place is to purchase or find suitable storage for them. You can simply use the drawer of your bedside table. However, if you don't have one available, you can create a dream box – use an attractive box, or one that you can paint or decorate yourself, or perhaps some other inspiring container of your choice. A dream box will add a personal and sentimental touch to your dream-recording practice. It will also help keep your journal private, and it serves as an organizational solution because it keeps all of your recording tools in one safe and easy-to-access place.

TRAVEL

I am often asked how to fit a conscious dreaming practice into the disruption of travelling. One easy remedy is to bring your dream journal on your travels and holidays. If you are concerned about misplacing your dream journal while away from home, you can purchase an easy-to-carry smaller journal that is specifically for documenting your dreams during your time away.

Your travelling dream journal can end up being a fun and creative project for your travels. You can title the journal based on the place you are visiting, for example, "Hawaiian dreams" or "Dream time in Australia". You can also get creative and make a visually-themed dream journal, with images and collage, or you can collect mementos from your holiday to put into the journal.

Being in a new place can often change a person's routine and lead to unique experiences that can trigger more inspired dreams. Being relaxed, connected to nature and stress-free on holidays can sometimes result in deeply connected, more insightful and more meaningful dreams. Travelling can be a great opportunity for you to reflect upon your inner worlds, to check in with your wellbeing and to be intuitively open to receive guidance from your subconscious mind.

Recording in your dream journal

How you keep your records will be up to you and what feels intuitive. Some dreamers are particularly detailed in their record-keeping, whereas others jot down only the key aspects. However, the more details you provide when writing out your dreams, the more clues and insight you will glean. As soon as you wake up, make a record of your dream. Be disciplined to do this first thing in the morning before visiting the bathroom or checking your smartphone. The dream will be fresh in your mind and any interruption could easily make it dissipate. As recording your dream becomes a solid morning ritual, you will find that your mind becomes trained for easier recall.

RECORD-KEEPING DETAILS

You should start each dream with brief record-keeping details such as the date and dream genre. These entries can help you to find a particular dream or establish patterns in your dreaming when you review your journal in the future. You can then follow these details with more detailed documentation of the dream as well as how you feel about it and your interpretation.

DATE
Write out the date: day, month and year. Some more detailed dreamers also include the time.

DREAM GENRE AND TYPE
Include the genre of your dream. Just like films have genres, such as a comedy or thriller, so do dreams! Was it a lucid dream, sleep paralysis, a precognitive dream or a recurring dream? Familiarize yourself with the various categories of dreams that you can experience (see page 100).

DREAM TITLE
Name your dream. Come up with a creative title for your dream as you would do for a film, book or song. Giving your dream a title will help you to personalize it, define it, bring it to life, bridge it over into your waking time and christen it as a creative work of art from your unconscious mind.

DOCUMENTING YOUR DREAM

As you write, flow out onto the pages of your journal the dream as it unfolded, from start to finish, and write down every little detail that you can remember. This includes all of the visual aspects of your dream, no matter how absurd or unimportant or even boring you may find them. Many a dreamer fails to record their mundane or bland dreams because they think they are not interesting enough to be of any importance. But even your monotonous dreams can often have messages or ideas for you.

Take your time to let the memory of the dream unfold and write it out. If you are in a morning rush and do not have the luxury of time to write an epic piece, simply jot down the key details of the dream in an outline form and return to it later for further elaboration.

Write with a flowing stream of consciousness. Do not be concerned about using the right words or developing a clever narrative. Your mission should be to get as many details written down as possible before you lose the dream.

EMOTIONS

As well as being filled with visual cues, dreams are emotive. The emotional atmosphere of the dream is one of the biggest clues to interpretation. Was the dream hilarious? Scary? Creepy? Confusing? Troubling? As you write out your dream, ask yourself: What were the mood and atmosphere like? How did you feel emotionally? Did your emotions evolve within the dream? Did it start off pleasant and turn into negativity or vice versa? Take note of any emotionally charged atmospheres or situations and articulate them and how they evolved in your documentations.

SETTING

Make sure that you give detailed descriptions of your dream setting. Perhaps it is a place that you know well, such as your childhood home, your workplace or a city you once visited. Conceivably, it could be an unknown place, a surreal city or a natural habitat of beauty or unfamiliarity. Try to provide as many details as you can to describe the dream environment.

There are often symbolisms that can help decode your dream. For example, a house typically symbolizes an aspect of your psyche, or "self". Water universally symbolizes your emotions or spiritual self.

ABSTRACTIONS

Did something abstract in the dream remind you of someone? Perhaps the appearance of a bird felt like your mother, or a person you took to be your father looked like a stranger. Perhaps someone or a situation came to mind even though the visuals of the dream did not match your thoughts. It is important to take note of the cognitive information of your dreams. They are big clues that can help you interpret your dream later on. Express this aspect in your documentation.

Some examples of communicating this abstraction are, "I found a wounded bird on the ground. For some reason it reminded me of my mother," or "A man in a military uniform was helping me find my car; he felt like he was supposed to be my father, but he didn't look like him at all."

SENSORY

When documenting your dream, make sure you include any details of colours, textures, shapes, sounds, aromas or physical actions. If you dreamed of a house, what colour was the house? If you dreamed your friend was wearing a large overcoat, what was the colour of the coat? Colours can be important symbols that can assist in dream interpretation. Be sure to document these details even though you may not find them important.

The same goes for physical actions. Were you flying in your dream? Running? Swimming? Physical movements in dreams are also symbolic and can provide important signals when you get down to interpreting them.

FOLLOWING UP ON YOUR DREAMS

After you write out your dream in its entirety, make room on the pages that proceed to write a follow-up. A follow-up includes your first-hand thoughts on how the dream made you feel and then a more in-depth analysis of the dream in the form of an interpretation.

MOOD

Begin your follow-up with the sentence: "This dream made me feel..." and fill in the blank. Did the dream make you feel anxious? Joyful? Fearful? Sad? Infuriated? Inspired? Hopeful? Your emotional response within the dream is one of the biggest clues you will receive for decoding it. It directly relates to feelings and emotions that your subconscious mind is processing and wants to bring to your attention.

Some dreams can feel confusing. A dream can appear sunny, happy and even beautiful and yet your emotional response may not match the visuals. For example, you can have a dream of a beautiful, outdoor summer wedding, where everyone is happy and celebrating, yet you have a feeling of deep anxiety or perhaps dread. There is a lot of information to be found in the contrasts of this dream example.

Perhaps it is a prompt for the dreamer to reflect on his or her feelings about relationship commitment or marriage.

INTENT

If you are engaged in your conscious dreaming practice, you should be setting intents each evening before you fall asleep. An intent is simply an aim or a goal that you would like to achieve in either your waking life or your dreamworld. Conscious dreamers set intents to gain insight or guidance from their dreams. It could be a practical goal such as, "I will find my own hands in my dreams tonight" (*also see* page 63), which assists in training your brain for lucid dreaming. Or the intent could be for problem-solving: "I will work out the code for that formula in my dreams tonight." Or it could be for emotional growth: "I will look for opportunities to emotionally heal in my dreams tonight."

INTERPRETATION

You may find that you prefer to do this at a later time, perhaps in the evening before you go to sleep, or during a reflective time in your day. Some dreamers will record an interpretation straight away because they feel quite clear about what they believe the dream symbolized. Yet, still, you may find that your dream is a challenging riddle to solve and it may take some time to do so. I know I have certainly had experiences where I was unable to interpret certain dreams until years later. The beauty of keeping a dream journal is that you can always go back at any point to reflect, ponder, decode and continue to learn from your dreams.

Some questions to ask yourself as you prepare to interpret your dream:

* What was the intent that I set for myself last night?

* Does it correlate to my dream in any way?

* What did I do yesterday and what was my emotional state?

* Does this influence or relate to my dream in any way?

* What are the current themes or challenges that I'm experiencing in my waking life?

* Do these influence or relate to my dream in any way?

RECURRING THEMES

There will be times when recurring themes appear in your weekly dreams. This is another important aspect of keeping a dream journal: it enables you to catch the similarities you experience in separate dreams. Perhaps you have a dream about a fox and then at two other times in the same month the fox makes an appearance. These recurrences are a great prompt to further investigate the symbolism of foxes (for more on Dream symbols see page 110).

The recurring themes do not necessarily have to be visual; they can be emotive or mood-based. Perhaps you had a whole week of nightmares or anxiety filled dreams. This is a signal for you to sit down and have a look at your current emotional state or perhaps your hidden and repressed feelings. The recurring themes of dreams are there to get your attention and guide you to look at the deeper aspects of your psyche and unconscious that you may or may not be neglecting. They recur because they are trying to get through to you.

REFLECTION

After you write down, follow up and interpret your dreams, it is time to mesh them into your waking life. A considerable amount of reflection is required to bridge any lessons or guidance you have received from your dreams into your daily life. Perhaps one of your dreams appears to be prompting you to speak up more at work when you feel like you have been treated unfairly, or perhaps some dreams are prompting you to resolve issues and mend bridges between you and a family member. Whatever the message or guidance, this is the chapter of conscious dreaming where we can make a difference in our lives and potentially the lives of others.

INTEGRATION

As we begin to bridge the lessons and guidance from our dreams into our waking lives, aspects of ourselves become more fully integrated. A balance between our unconscious and conscious minds begins to even out and communicate freely in awareness of each other. This helps us during our waking moments to be more conscious, mindful and aware of the undercurrents of our subconscious behaviour and, in turn, it helps us to manage them more effectively. This can bring a sense of wholeness and wellness to the individual and a sense of knowing oneself.

Dream plants and herbs

It seems that the busy, noisy and distracted components of modern, consumerist culture is causing a number of people to experience a disconnect from nature and the natural world. These people are increasingly dedicating more time to their smartphones than to being in their gardens or local parks.

If you have an increased disconnect from nature and the natural world, it will keep you disconnected from the quiet of your mind and dreams. In the wise and timely words of the indigenous North American Lakota tribe: "When a man moves away from nature, his heart becomes hard." With this in mind, it is worth mentioning another important aspect of a conscious dreaming practice: your reconnection to nature.

Reconnecting to nature

One of the most effective ways to reconnect with nature is through plants. By developing a relationship with a few herbs and dream plants, you can begin to work in partnership with them to bring about more vivid dream states, improve dream recall and have more meaningful, guidance-based dreams on a regular basis.

Plants that help with dreaming are considered to be "oneirogens". The term is a combination of the Greek words *oneiros*, which means "dream", and *gen*, which translates as "to create".

The fundamental key to working with oneirogens is to consider these plants as guides. With this role in mind, you can form a partnership based on respect, balance, gratitude and love. In the words of the Native American Arapaho tribe: "All plants are our brothers and sisters. They talk to us and if we listen, we can hear them."

Dream tea ritual

If drinking herbal tea is for you and you want to incorporate dream plants into your conscious dreaming practice, you can establish a dream tea ritual before you go to sleep. Dream plants can improve your dream recall, trigger more dreams and assist you with any advance dream work that you are engaging in, such as lucid dreaming, mutual dreaming and precognitive dreams. It's good to note that, like all things, it's best to use herbs and dream plants in moderation. Test what works for you but refrain from going overboard!

SAFETY FIRST

When incorporating new herbs and dream plants into your life, it is important to consider several factors. Like all plants, they can produce allergic reactions in susceptible people. They should not be taken if you are pregnant, and some of these plants have not been fully tested and approved. Some herbs and dream plants can counteract with, and be dangerous if used in combination with, prescription drugs, antidepressants, alcohol or sedatives. You should take herbs and dream plants with care and under the supervision of a healthcare provider.

PREPARING AN OVER-THE-COUNTER DREAM TEA

The first step to preparing a dream tea is choosing a herb or dream plant. The following is a list of tested everyday, sleepy herbal teas that aid in relaxation and dreaming time (for more on Dream plants, *see* page 88):

Lemon balm

Chamomile

Valerian root

Lavender

You are now ready to start your dream tea ritual:

✳ Prepare the herb in a cup or teapot and add boiling water.

✳ Allow the herb to infuse for 10 minutes.

✳ Add any desired sweetener, such as honey or agave syrup.

✳ Sit in quiet, meditative reflection.

✳ With mindful intent for dreaming, drink your dream tea.

✳ Settle to bed, keeping your dreaming intent in mind and fall into a meditative sleep.

A guide to dream plants

There are many exotic types of dream plants that come from all over the world. They each have their own historical and cultural background and unique qualities that help perfume the nature of dreams. In this section we will take a closer look at five of these dream plants.

Remember that if you want to use dream plants, you should take them with care and under the supervision of a healthcare provider (*see* Safety first on page 86), and they should not be taken if you are pregnant.

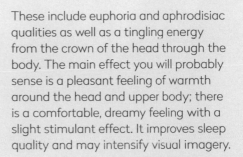

BLUE LOTUS

Nymphaea caerulea

For more than three thousand years the blue lotus was used by the priesthood of ancient Egypt for its medicinal properties and as a spiritual sacrament. The plant was regarded as the symbol of the sun and played an important part in Egyptian mythology. The walls of the famous Egyptian temple of Karnak feature many blue lotus flowers in scenes of magical rites, celebration and rites of passage into the afterlife.

The blue lotus generally produces mild psychoactive effects that are purported to have a "divine" essence that brings on the feelings of tranquillity and subtle euphoria. Today, it is used by herbalists to treat insomnia, but it has also been reported to induce lucid dreaming

The mildly sedating effects and appearance of the blue lotus flower make it a likely candidate for the lotus plant eaten by the mythical Lotophagi ("lotus-eaters") in Homer's *Odyssey*.

USE
Make into a tea by adding several petals to hot water and infusing for 10 minutes.

EFFECTS
Contains the psychoactive alkaloid apomorphine and causes sedation. The effects can be felt after one cup of tea.

These include euphoria and aphrodisiac qualities as well as a tingling energy from the crown of the head through the body. The main effect you will probably sense is a pleasant feeling of warmth around the head and upper body; there is a comfortable, dreamy feeling with a slight stimulant effect. It improves sleep quality and may intensify visual imagery.

CAUTIONS
Do not take if you are pregnant.
Do not drive or operate heavy machinery.
Do not mix with medicines.

ALLERGIES
It is possible to have an allergic reaction to blue lotus. Conduct an allergy skin patch test or use under the supervision of your healthcare provider.

LEGAL STATUS
Blue lotus is uncontrolled in the UK and the US. This means all parts of the plant and its extracts are legal to cultivate, buy, possess and distribute (sell, trade or give) without a license or prescription. If sold as a supplement, sales must conform to UK and US supplement laws. It is illegal in Poland, Latvia and Russia.

DREAM HERB

Calea zacatechichi/C. ternifolia

The Chontal Indians of the Oaxaca region in Mexico have a long tradition of using dream herb for their dreams. They call it *thle-pelakano*, meaning the "leaf of god". It is also known as bitter leaf and bitter grass because of its bitingly bitter taste when consumed as tea.

For the Chontal Indians, the leaf of god enables the ability to obtain insight and sharpen intuitive perception in dreams. It also helps to increase dreaming and to induce lucid dreams. The Chontal Indians prepare *thle-pelakano* by brewing up a powerful tea with the dried leaves. They drink the tea, relax and smoke the dried leaves just before they go to sleep. A handful of about 60g (2oz) of dried herbage is considered an effective dosage.

C. zacatechichi has been scientifically shown to increase dream recall, dream intensity and hypnagogic imagery. It has also been used in folk remedies for thousands of years as an appetite stimulant, cleansing agent, calming agent, laxative and for the treatment of diarrhoea, dysentery, fever, skin rashes, swollen scalps and headaches.

The plant has been tentatively identified as one of the plants adorning Aztec statues of Xochipilli.

USE
Make into a tea; to ease the bitterness of the tea, add honey or agave syrup.

EFFECTS
Intensification of visual imagery during hypnagogic states and sleep.

CAUTIONS
Do not take if you are pregnant.

ALLERGIES
It is possible to have an allergic reaction to dream herb. Conduct an allergy patch skin test or use under the supervision of your healthcare provider.

LEGAL STATUS
Often sold as *Calea zacatechichi*, dream herb is uncontrolled in the UK and the US. This means all parts of the plant and its extracts are legal to cultivate, buy, possess and distribute (sell, trade or give) without a licence or prescription. If sold as a supplement, sales must conform to UK and US supplement laws. It is illegal in Poland.

GUAYUSA

Ilex guayusa

Guayusa (pronounced gwai-yoo-sa) has been a big part of the dream work traditions of the Kichwa people of the Amazon. In the Ecuadorian rainforest, before sunrise, leaves from the guayusa tree are collected and boiled in a large pot known as a *guayucero*. After the leaves have brewed, the members of the Kichwa community share a *pilche* (a hollowed-out wooden bowl or cup) filled with guayusa. They sit around the fire, drinking the tea and discussing and interpreting their dreams. The Kichwa take their dreams seriously. The dream they have the night before is specifically used for guiding them the next day.

When early European colonialists asked the Indigenous people how they obtained their knowledge of the uses of certain plants, a common response was "the plants told us". In Kichwa legends, there is a story of twins who went in search of a plant that would teach them how to dream. After they fell asleep, they dreamed of meeting their ancestors, who gifted them guayusa leaves. When they awoke, they were still clutching the plants in their hands.

Archaeological evidence suggests the plant has been used and traded in the greater Andes-Amazon region since at least 500CE.

USE
Make into a tea using five leaves per cup and infusing for 10 minutes.

EFFECTS
Guayusa is naturally packed with polyphenols and caffeine; it has less caffeine than coffee and twice as many antioxidants as green tea.

CAUTIONS
Do not take if you are pregnant.

ALLERGIES
It is possible to have an allergic reaction to guayusa. Conduct an allergy skin patch test or use under the supervision of your healthcare provider.

MUGWORT

Artemisia vulgaris

Also known as common wormwood, mugwort is a wild and abundant plant whose genus name of *Artemisia* is named for the Greek moon goddess and patron of womanly health, Artemis.

The North American Chumash Indians referred to mugwort as dream sage and used it for hundreds of years to promote dreaming. The Paiute name is translated as "dream plant".

USE
Make into a tea by infusing for 10 minutes.

EFFECTS
Apart from the intensification of visual imagery during sleep, you may find yourself experiencing a sense of wellbeing, light-headedness and clarity the day after.

Mugwort contains thujone (an active chemical compound in the spirit absinthe), which can be toxic if consumed in large amounts or for prolonged periods.

ALLERGIES
It is possible to have an allergic reaction to mugwort. Conduct an allergy skin patch test or use under the supervision of your healthcare-provider.

PASSIONFLOWER

Passiflora incarnata

Long before it was "discovered" by the Spanish in 1569, indigenous tribes throughout the Amazon used passionflower for its various medicinal qualities. They called it *maracuja*.

The Christian missionaries gave the flower its current name to help spread the message of their religion. They found it easier to connect with the indigenous tribes by using the realms of nature and symbolism and explained to them that each part of the flower holds symbolic meaning in recognition of the Crucifixion story – the Passion of Christ.

Since its introduction into European herbal medicine systems, passionflower has been widely used as a sedative, antispasmodic and nerve tonic. In many countries in Europe, the US and Canada, the use of dried passionflower leaves has been documented for more than two hundred years. It was also employed for colic, diarrhoea, dysentery, menstrual difficulties, insomnia, neuralgia, eye disorders, epilepsy and convulsions, and muscle spasms and pain.

Most *Passiflora* species grow in South America and in tropical zones. Around 40 species grow in Asia, Madagascar, Australia and the South Pacific Islands.

Passionflower leaves are classified as "Generally Regarded as Safe" by the US Food and Drug Administration (FDA).

USE
Make into a tea by infusing leaves for 10 minutes.

EFFECTS
It can cause drowsiness or have a tranquillizing effect.

CAUTIONS
Do not take if you are pregnant.

ALLERGIES
It is possible to have an allergic reaction to passionflower. Conduct an allergy patch skin test or use under the supervision of your healthcare provider.

Hypnagogic meditation

Every night when you fall asleep, your sleep cycle kicks in and you slip into the hypnagogic state (*see* page 22). You will not be fully asleep or fully awake but hovering in that liminal space on the threshold. If, during this phase, you are able to hold onto your awareness and observe what is unfolding in your mind's eye, you may experience all sorts of imagery, sights and even sounds. It often takes some self-discipline to hold onto awareness in this liminal state, because your body is slipping into sleep, but nonetheless it is a worthwhile experiment to engage in.

There are several ways you can train your mind to observe and learn from the hypnagogic state. It can help you become a more conscious dreamer. One effective way to train yourself to be aware of the images that unfold in your mind's eye is to engage in a hypnagogic meditation during the day when wide awake.

BENEFITS OF HYPNAGOGIC MEDITATION

This simple daily visual meditation will help you to:

✳ Become more present, observant and aware within a dream state.

✳ Train your mind's eye to see and understand the visual language of dreams.

✳ Train yourself to observe without emotional attachment, just like you would observe a film or video clip.

✳ Become aware of visually repetitive themes and concepts.

✳ Begin to understand the visual metaphors and symbolisms of dream state visuals.

STEPS FOR HYPNAGOGIC MEDITATION

To practise hypnagogic meditation, set aside 10–20 minutes of your day. Find a quiet place where you will not be disturbed or interrupted. You may want to use an alarm to indicate when it is time to end your meditation.

* Sit comfortably and quietly.

* Close your eyes.

* Focus on your breathing.

* Let your body settle.

* Observe your emotions.

* Feel them in your body.

* Visualize letting them go.

* Observe the chatter in your mind.

* Visualize letting the thoughts go.

* Settle into the present moment.

* With eyes closed, softly fix your gaze on the dark background behind your eyelids, like watching a film screen.

* Just observe – do not think too much about it.

* Observe what visually unfolds.

* Do not try to analyse it, just let it flow and observe what you see.

* Do not emotionally attach yourself to the visuals that unfold.

* Let the images continue to evolve until your alarm rings (if using one) or you are ready to stop.

* Slowly come back into the present moment.

* Open your eyes.

* Slowly move your limbs and body.

* Record the visuals you observed in your dream journal.

What you see or observe in your mind's eye during your hypnagogic meditation will probably be surreal and random. In your dream journal, record what you observed, felt or sensed. By learning how to observe your visual hypnagogia, you will also find a way in which to transition into a Lucid dream (see page 132).

Dream sharing

Another important element of your conscious dreaming practice is to actively share your dreams with others. This can help you with interpretation, processing, problem-solving, creativity, dream memory recall, emotional integration and triggering more dreams. It is also a great way to connect with other dreamers, build new relationships, inspire others and receive some support and encouragement with your practice.

An ancient practice

Sharing dreams is not a new idea. People have been sharing their dreams for thousands of years. There are records dating as far back as at least 4000–3000BCE. In ancient Egypt, dreams were among the items recorded in the form of hieroglyphics. In ancient Egyptian culture, dream sharing had a religious context with priests doubling as dream interpreters.

The respect for dreams changed radically early in the 19th century, when dreams were thought to be influenced by anxiety, the surrounding environment and the food you ate. During this chapter of history, there was less interest in dreams and the popularity of dream interpretation somewhat dissipated.

However, with the arrival later in the 19th century of Sigmund Freud, a big advocate of the importance of dreams, the art of dream interpretation made a comeback. Today, there are a number of different ways in which you can share your dreams. Simply choose the methods that are more suited to you.

Creativity and dream sharing

You can share your dreams through your creative practice. Countless works of music and art have come from the realms of dreaming. Jimi Hendrix wrote the 1967 song "Purple Haze" based on a dream in which he walked under the sea before a purple haze surrounded him. Salvador Dali placed great importance on his dreams, which can be seen in his 1933 surrealist painting *The Dream*. Edgar Allan Poe had nightmares throughout his life that inspired his short stories and poems. His most notable poems about dreaming are "Dream-Land" and "A Dream Within a Dream".

Your dream journal is the perfect source of creative inspiration. Read through your dreams and see if any inspiration unfolds. Perhaps a nightmare could be manifested into a painting, or perhaps a lucid dream into a piece of music. If you are a filmmaker, you can translate a surreal dream into a brilliant scene in a film. There are countless creative ways to evolve the experiences of your dreams. Sharing your dreams in these creative ways can bring inspiration and emotive responses to your audience.

Inspiration for ideas

Perhaps it is not a creative practice that compels you to share your dreams. It could simply be ideas, theories, problem-solving solutions or inventions. There are countless examples of people throughout history who shared ideas from their dreams and changed the course of humanity. For example: a young Albert Einstein had a dream that he was speeding down a steep and snowy hill on a sled. As he approached the speed of light, the colours and surroundings all blended into one. Einstein reflected and meditated on this dream and its inspiration would eventually lead to him working out his theory of relativity: one of the most significant scientific contributions of the 20th century.

Social media

Instagram, Facebook, Twitter, dream forums... there are many ways you can share your dreams online. You can share dream journal excerpts, images you find online that resemble an aspect of your dream, your experiences with sleep paralysis, recurring dreams and symbols that appear in your dreams.

Sharing online will connect you with other dreamers and it's likely you will find that people generally respond with intrigue to dreams. People will often relate and communicate that they have experienced something similar. It is a great way to expand your experience of dreaming into your waking life. You will meet a lot of like-minded explorers and receive the connections and support that help you along with your conscious dreaming practice.

Dream friends

Find yourself a friend that is also exploring his or her dreams and regularly share your dreams with each other. Having another dreamer as a sounding board can greatly help with interpretation and seeing the bigger picture of the dream. A dream comrade can also offer insight, support and intuitive guidance regarding the dreams that you share. Dream friends are also great for experimenting with Mutual dreams (*see* page 138).

Dream circles

These are safe places in which people meet up regularly to openly discuss and share their dreams. Ideas, techniques, theories and tips are also shared and discussed. If you cannot find one where you live, you can start your own dream circle with a few friends. It is important to share your dreams with other caring and supportive dreamers who can help you unlock their meanings, delight in and share their synchronicities, and help hold the space for exploration and wonder. This will help with a deeper connectivity not only to yourself but to those within your circle and beyond.

Dream circles develop a unique and wonderful energy of their own. In the regular dream circles that I have held, we often found ourselves in each other's dreams and often with similar themes. It is also a great space in which to receive feedback, encourage your conscious dreaming practice, keep on top of your dream journaling, and experiment with various lucid dreaming and mutual dreaming techniques (*see* pages 132 and 138). Dreaming workshops and retreats are also immersive ways in which to share and explore dreams.

THE FOUNDATIONS OF A CONSCIOUS DREAMING PRACTICE

HOW TO START A DREAM CIRCLE

If you want to start up your own dream circle, announce it to your friends. Ideally, four to ten people are enough, because a small goup will allow more time for sharing. Organization will be necessary to get the group going, starting with finding a regular meet-up spot. Some groups take it in turn to meet in their own homes.

When running a group, consider the following suggestions:

* Establish a consistent schedule either weekly, biweekly or monthly.

* Allow 2–3 hours for each meeting to give enough time to share and explore the dreams.

* Encourage each member to commit to recording dreams in a dream journal.

* Ask each member to bring a dream journal to the circle for sharing and discussion.

* Create a peaceful and comfortable space for the circle; it could literally mean sitting in a circle on the floor or sitting on comfortable furniture. A warming environment of candles, tea and aromatherapy can help create a calming mood for sharing dreams.

* Open the circle by introducing yourself and sharing a dream. It could be a dream from the previous night or perhaps a profound dream from previous years that has left a lasting impression on you.

* Encourage the group to discuss and explore each other's dreams.

* Be sure to keep things moving around the circle.

* Take note and discuss your own conscious dreaming progress and the progress of the group at each new meeting.

* Set tasks, goals and participate in experimenting with new techniques.

PART 4

Dream Genres

Why distinguish dream genres?

The types of dreams you have can be categorized by genres, much in the same way as comedy, horror, thriller, romance and other genres are used to identify different types of films. Recognizing the different categories of dreams that you experience will help you tremendously when navigating, exploring and engaging with your conscious dreaming practice. Being able to understand how these dream genres play out, their themes and their underpinning will link you to your unconscious mind and make your dream journaling, reflections and analysis much easier. It will also assist you in implementing and integrating valuable insight and guidance into your waking life and can help encourage you to further explore your dreaming time as a oneironaut.

Compensatory dreams

Although compensatory dreams are often mistaken for prophetic dreams, in reality they are dreams with subliminal messages. They occur to get our attention to help balance out an aspect of our psyche in waking life.

The first use of the term "compensatory dreams"

The Swiss psychiatrist and psychoanalyst Carl Jung coined the term "compensatory dreams". He believed that dreams are compensatory, which in essence means that they compensate for emotions, perceptions and thoughts that are experienced but are either repressed or not strong enough to reach consciousness. These emotions, perceptions and thoughts that never make it to the consciousness lay dormant in the unconscious and therefore find their way into dreams, as a result manifesting in the language of symbols. Dreams are a way for the psyche to self-regulate.

Shy people can often reveal their extrovert side in a dream, whereas people with an uptight personality may find themselves laughing hysterically nonstop in a dream. Compensatory dreams are useful in altering yourself to a given situation. These dreams are highly personal and emerge in different ways to each person, so it is important to reflect upon which part of your conscious action and attitude these dreams are seeking to compensate.

The shadow

Another important element of understanding your compensatory dreams is the Jungian concept of "the shadow". The shadow is your dark side, all the negative aspects of yourself that you do not want to identify with or are not fully conscious of. The notion of this theory is that the more you ignore or repress your shadow, the more it seeks to boil over. In other words, the suppressed shadow will eventually rear its ugly head to get your attention, in order for you to transcend it, transform it and integrate it. Ultimately, it is for balance within your psyche and soul.

Your shadow, or dark side, will often appear in compensatory dreams or nightmares (see page 124). These occurrences are great prompts and opportunities for you to look deeper into your subconscious machinations. In what is known as shadow work, you actively embrace your nightmares to transcend and positively integrate the shadowy aspects of your psyche.

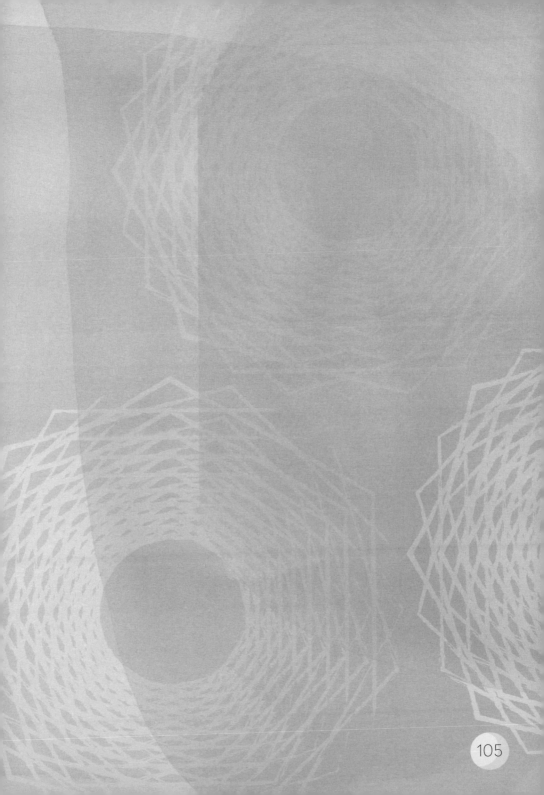

105

Decoding your dreams

Like all dreamers, you have the ability to decode your own dreams. As a conscious dreamer, unlocking a compensatory dream is done through self-analysis. Your dream journal plays a particularly important role, as your recorded dreams will enable you to reflect, examine and unpack the contents of your compensatory dreams. It will allow you to recognize the clear messages in your dreams that are prompting you to make the necessary changes in your waking life.

It can feel transcendent when you are able to unlock the meaning of your dreams. Having personal "Eureka!" moments can be enlightening experiences of self-actualization and consciousness development.

Sometimes it is easier said than done! Compensatory dreams can at times be deeply symbolic and confusing. Archetypal and mythological figures that appear within dreams can be complex. It is important to be aware of your emotional responses with such dreams and apply them to your analysis.

STEPS TO DECODING YOUR COMPENSATORY DREAMS

✳ Write down your dream upon awakening.

✳ Analyse the scene that unfolded in your dream. For example:

"I was walking down the street and saw a man walking toward me. I did not know who he was nor did I recognize him. All of a sudden, out of nowhere, I felt compelled to verbally and physically attack him."

✳ Was your behaviour in your dream different from how you are in waking life? Take note of any differences. For example:

"In my dream I attacked this innocent man. For no reason at all, I felt full of murderous rage. I was hitting him and beating him up. This is absolutely not something I would do in my waking life. I'm a peaceful, loving person and I don't like confrontations!"

✳ How did this behaviour make you feel? Explore your emotional response more deeply and write down any insight. For example:

"In my dream I felt out of control and full of hate. I felt like I was evil or something. I woke up feeling really guilty and feeling like I was a bad person for verbally and physically attacking that innocent man!"

✳ Now reflect on the dream symbols and abstractions that appeared in your dream. For example:

"The only dream symbol that comes to mind is this man."

✳ Write down any intuitive insight that you receive regarding any dream symbols and abstractions. For example:

"I think the innocent man in my dream might represent men in general, or perhaps my overall feelings toward men. It could also possibly represent my masculine side."

✳ Reflect on any insights, messages, guidance or lessons that you receive from your decoded dream. For example:

"I think I feel like I might have a lot of suppressed rage and disdain when it comes to men. I have been hurt a lot in the past and harassed a lot by men on the street, but I have never spoken up for myself. I always avoid

*confrontation and I have not dealt
with the emotional fallout of some of
my more painful relationships. I tend
to just ignore it and squish my feelings
down. I think this dream is prompting
me to look at these repressed
emotions so that I can transcend
them and change the way I have been
relating to men in my waking life."*

✳ Write down how you intend to
integrate the lessons of your dream
in your waking reality. For example:

*"I will be more conscious in my waking
life of my emotional triggers when it
comes to men. If something reminds
me of painful past relationships, I will
sit with the emotions, meditate on
them and observe them instead of
squishing them down deep inside
of me. I will make a concerted
effort to face and embrace these
challenging emotions and transcend
my negative views of men."*

✳ Integrate the dream experience into
your waking life by committing to
follow through with your above
intentions of being more conscious,
navigating through challenging
emotions and implementing positive
change where it needs to happen.

Dream symbols

Through cultivating a dreaming practice you can begin to understand the rich meaning of symbols within your dreams. Dream symbols can sometimes be universal or especially personal, and great discernment is required to decode the messages of your own dreams. Understanding your own personal symbolisms will come through dream journaling, reflection, meditation, synchronicity and personal experience.

Universal dream symbols

Symbols are the language of dreams. Feelings and ideas can often be invoked through symbols that prompt the dreamer to act on solving the deeper meaning of their mystery. Cultivating the ability to interpret your own dreams is a powerful tool. Because dreams are so personal and integral to your own psyche and unconscious mind, no one is more expert at interpreting your own dreams than yourself.

There is a plethora of information out there on dream symbols and dream interpretations. Now, with a simple Google search, a perplexed dreamer can quickly begin decoding the meanings of their complex, curiously symbolic dreams. Of course, these universal interpretations might not necessarily be the final conclusion, but they can be used as guidance for your exploration and offer a helpful starting point for unpicking your own dreams.

12 UNIVERSAL DREAM SYMBOLS AND THEIR MEANINGS

Animals	Basic instincts, behaviours and emotions
Desert	Loss, loneliness, left behind
Feet	Foundations, stability
Fire	Purification, transformation, anger, passion, destruction
Hair	Personal power, strength, virility
Hands	Self-expression, communication, how you connect with the world
House	Self, psyche
Key	Unlocking answers, freedom, secrets revealed, new opportunities
Pregnancy and babies	New ideas, new creative project, new possibilities and potential for growth
Road	Life journey, life path, direction
Sex	Desire for emotional intimacy and connection, merging aspects of self (masculine/feminine)
Vehicles	Direction life is taking you, your physical body, mind or ego
Water	Emotions, unconscious mind, spirituality

ANIMAL

SYMBOLISM

Dreams that involve animal symbolism can be surprisingly easy to interpret. Some of the questions to ask yourself are: what are the characteristics of the animal? Personality type? Physical attributes? Strengths and weaknesses? These elements can be directly applied to the overall theme or deeper message of your dream.

Personal symbolism

When analysing your dreams, consider every microscopic detail of the dream: emotions, atmosphere, associations. Closely look at the details such as objects, colour, numbers, people and places. Even if a person does not appear in your dream but merely comes to mind, it can hold some significance; for example, if a rabbit in your dream makes you think of your mother. It is important to take note of the emotions that you experience in the context of the dream. How did you feel when you saw the rabbit that reminded you of your mother? These are big clues.

Using online dream dictionaries along with your own personal intuition, experiences, history, circumstances and memory can be an enormous guide for interpreting your own dream in an integrally deep and personal way. Interpreting and understanding the cryptic symbolism of your own dreams can help evolve your own personal mythology. Like all dreamers, you will grapple with your own highly personal mythology – the psychic force that allows you to weave the fragments of your experience into a coherent story.

Personal mythology

Personal mythology is your own inner story. It is important to live life with a knowledge of its mystery and your own mystery. It gives life a new zest, a new balance and new harmony. Thinking in mythological terms can help you see the symbolism of your dreams and inner worlds and how they reflect and play out in your external life.

DEVELOPING YOUR OWN PERSONAL MYTHOLOGY

To explore and evolve as a conscious dreamer, embracing the symbols within your dreams and bridging them over, into your waking life, can bring you clarity, purpose, a stronger connection with yourself and maybe even some lovely new jewellery. (I always buy a silver pendant or a ring of the symbols in my dreams.)

Here are some steps to get you on your way to exploring and then implementing your own personal mythology:

* Read your dream journals.

* Look for recurring themes, characters or symbols.

* Gather information.

* Research the symbols you find in your recorded dreams.

* Reflect on their meanings and your intuitive response.

* Write your findings in your dream journal.

* Get creative: draw, sketch, paint or make a collage of your personal dream symbols; collect images of your personal dream symbols to print out; look online for pendants or objects that represent your dream symbols and purchase them.

* Integrate: reflect on the meaning of your personal dream symbols in the greater context of your life.

PERSONAL REMINDERS

Here is an example of how a personal mythology might develop. You have a recurring dream theme of wolves and have noted this and researched the symbolism of the wolf. In your research you have found that wolves symbolize personal power, self-control and instincts. Then you sit down and think about the wolf in the context of you and your life. When you think of your life as a myth, you can relate to the personality of the wolf. After all, you feel like you have always been a loner. At times in your life you have felt disempowered, so the symbol of the wolf's self-power brings you encouragement, aspiration and inspiration. You decide to buy a wolf ring to remind yourself of your own personal mythology. Wearing the ring serves as a reminder of the symbolisms of your own personal myth and journey.

MY SPIDER DREAMS:
A CASE STUDY

I have a recurring dream symbol of spiders. My records include countless dreams where I'm in awe of a giant spider weaving its web or where I am protecting a beautifully exotic spider from harm. These dreams have prompted me to investigate the deeper meaning of its symbolism and how I can apply it to my waking life. An example of one of these dreams is given here.

SPIDER DREAM
16 September 2017
I was walking through an unusual shop in East London. A bit of an art space. I walked into an empty room. There was a huge web. I felt in awe of how intricate it was. I saw writing on the floor but could not quite read it. Suddenly, an enormous spider appeared above me. It was black, hairy and had blue markings on its back. I was startled but not afraid. I was awestruck and mesmerized. I watched the silken threads flowing from the spider making the web. I was witnessing an important work of art.

SPIDER SYMBOL
In dreams, the symbol of the spider is generally associated with the archetype of the feminine, holding such qualities as receptivity, patience and creativity. It has also been associated with death and rebirth along with representing:

* Strong feminine energy

* Totemic symbol of the Mother

* Lunar symbol, ties in with the waxing and waning of the moon

* Polarity and balance

* Acts of creation such as writing

* Weaving a web of thoughts, ideas and actions

* The goddess of the Divine Mother, Neith in ancient Egypt

* Grandmother (to the Native Americans), linking the past to the future

* The symbol of infinity, given its figure-of-eight-shaped body

* Spiral energy and links with the past and future.

PERSONAL INTEGRATION
While writing this book, I continued to have recurring dream themes of spiders weaving webs. I decided to let my dreams inspire me and help with the writing process. I used the wall in my living room to create a giant "web" out of coloured masking tape and book writing notes. This dream inspired the creation on my wall and, in turn, helped me to navigate through my web of ideas and eventually structure them to become this book.

Recurring dreams

Dream themes that keep returning over and over again or dreams that you repeatedly experience over a long period of time are referred to as recurring dreams. These dreams can be either pleasant or nightmarish, and they can hold big clues about what your subconscious mind is trying to tell you.

Like most people, you probably have experienced a recurring dream in a chapter of your life. Most people are prone to such occurrences during childhood and then notice that they dissipate when entering adulthood. You may be able to relate to one of the more common recurring dream themes such as of teeth falling out, being chased, being unable to find a toilet when desperately needing one or being naked in a public place.

Much like nightmares, recurring dreams can appear during stressful and challenging times in your life. However, not all recurring dreams are nightmarish. Some are sublime, mysterious and even beautiful. So the fact that they are recurring is not necessarily a problem. They can feel somewhat transcendent or spiritual and their recurring aspect can be welcomed.

SIX COMMON RECURRING DREAMS AND THEIR MEANINGS

Being chased	Avoiding an issue, avoiding emotional fears or pain, skirting responsibility, feelings of guilt or shame
Falling from a great height	Feeling overwhelmed and out of control, insecure, anxious
Late for work	Fear of lack of control in career, fear of change, feeling disorganized
Teeth falling out	Fear of ageing, death, loss
Naked in public	Feelings of vulnerability, shame, hiding something
Water and drowning	Physical and emotional stress, fear of becoming overwhelmed by emotions

Theories behind recurring dreams

Recurring dreams are thought to occur because of unresolved stressors in a person's life, repressed emotional trauma, fears and phobias, post-traumatic stress disorder (PTSD) or obsessive-compulsive disorder (OCD). Evidence suggests that recurring dreams take place during times of stress, and when the problem has been resolved, these dreams will cease.

Some theories suggest that recurring dreams are a sort of "script", and as soon as a regular dream touches any aspect of the theme, the full script unfolds in completion of the recurring dream.

Much like a film, a recurring dream follows a script. When you have a recurring dream, it is effectively a film you have seen before. Because you are both the writer and director of your dreams, you have the ability to change the script.

Some people believe that recurring dreams are memories of past lives and that they hold unique qualities such as historical details and explanations for emotional and physical issues. They believe these dreams recur in order to heal and transcend the issues of that past incarnation.

STEPS TO DECODING YOUR RECURRING DREAMS

Many people can go their entire lives having the same dream and never understand its mystery. As a conscious dreamer, the key is to wake up to the dream by doing some reflection, inner work and decoding. Your recurring dream is specific only to you, and you are the only person who can innately unpick the symbols and deeper meaning and ultimately solve the mystery.

Recurring dreams are your unconscious mind telling you to wake up and address the problem. As with compensatory dreams, there are big messages for you to take action on, in order to face your shadow side and balance and integrate aspects of your psyche.

Solving the mystery of your recurring dream will take some reflective and investigative inner work. So grab your dream journal and a pen, sit down in a quiet and comfortable place, and immerse yourself in these steps:

✳ Write down the details of your recurring dream in your dream journal. This is the script of your recurring dream film.

✳ Analyse the scene that unfolded in your dream. For example:

"I was walking through my grandmother's house. I reached the stairs and started to climb up them. Things started feeling really weird and spooky. I started to get a queasy feeling in my stomach. I then saw the door at the top of the stairs open up and a really slow-moving scary-looking zombie cat came crawling out. I then suddenly began to feel that the teeth in my mouth were all coming loose, breaking apart and falling out. I totally freaked out and woke up."

✳ What emotions or bodily sensations did you feel in your dream?

✳ Explore more deeply your emotional response to these symbols or abstractions and write down any insight. For example:

"I felt creeped out, with a sense of dread in the pit of my stomach like something bad would happen. I felt morbid fear and disgust when I saw the zombie cat. I felt totally shocked and anxious when my teeth were falling out."

* Analyse any symbols or abractions within the dream.

* Now reflect on the dream symbols and abstractions that appeared in your dream.

* Write down any intuitive insight that you receive regarding any dream symbols and abstractions. For example:

"I feel like this might have to do with my grandmother because I am in her house. The door that opens at the top of the stairs is her bedroom, so I think it must be related to her. The cat, I feel, is a feminine symbol. The fact that it is a zombie feels like it symbolizes death. My teeth falling out feels like it represents loss."

* Reflect and write down any insights, messages, guidance or lessons that you receive from your decoded dream. For example:

"I feel like this recurring dream might have something to do with the fact that I am really scared of my grandmother dying and losing her."

* Write down how you intend to integrate the lessons of your dream in your waking reality. For example:

"I will be more conscious in my waking life about my feelings toward death and dying and will actively try to explore and express these feelings. I would like to get over the fear of death and I would like to be able to face the eventuality of my grandmother's death in a more conscious and positive way. I now intend to spend more time with my grandmother because I love her so much and she is so important to me. I want to make use of the precious time we have together."

* Integrate the dream experience into your waking life by committing to follow through with your above intentions of being more conscious, navigating through challenging emotions and implementing positive change where it needs to happen.

Nightmares

Ahh, the nightmare – the manifestion of your own personal horror film. This is the most unpleasant and creepy genre of dream you can experience. Even people who struggle with dream recall will most definitely remember a nightmare. In fact, some people can still recount vivid details of nightmares they had when they were small children. Nightmares trigger strong, negative, emotional responses that are typically related to anxiety, fear and despair.

Terrifying dreams

Throughout human history, nightmares were considered the work of demons and incubi. Countless works of art and folklore depict such entities crawling into the rooms of unexpecting sleepers, haunting and terrorizing them as they sleep. In Old English, the name of these creatures was *mare* or *mære* (from a proto-Germanic marōn, cf. Old Norse mara), hence comes the "*mare*" in the word "nightmare".

Nightmares occur during rapid eye movement (REM) sleep (*see* page 26), and they usually play out scenes of physical or psychological terror or situations of discomfort. Like most people, you may have experienced the sudden waking up from sleep with the feelings of distress, fear and anxiousness of a nightmare that makes it challenging for you to fall back asleep.

Nightmares can be so unpleasant that you may wonder, "Why me?", but if you begin to see them in a different light, you can learn a lot about what is going on with your physical and psychological wellbeing.

POTENTIAL CAUSES
OF NIGHTMARES

Nightmares can be triggered by a number of different causes, including the ones listed below:

✳ Abnormal sleep cycles.

✳ Stimulants or excessive alcohol consumption.

✳ Recent withdrawal from a medicine, such as sleeping pills, or abrupt alcohol withdrawal.

✳ Some medications and prescription drugs (including recreational drug use), or an adverse reaction to, or a side effect of, a medicine.

✳ Eating just before going to bed (because it raises the body's metabolism and brain activity).

✳ Mental health disorders, including post-traumatic stress disorder (PTSD).

✳ Breathing disorders during sleep (sleep apnoea).

✳ Sleep disorders (narcolepsy, sleep terror disorder).

✳ Sleeping in a supine position (on your back).

✳ Anxiety, bereavement or major life events.

✳ Dysfunction in REM sleep.

✳ Fever or illness.

Sleep paralysis

Some of my most terrifying sleep experiences have been during the state of sleep paralysis. Frozen between wakefulness and sleep, a sleep paralysis episode includes hearing sounds of buzzing, humming, static, zapping and hissing. Other creepy sounds include whispering voices, rushing and roaring wind sounds. Some people experience bodily sensations of electricity or vibrations through their bodies, floating out of body, feelings of sexual arousal and even sensations of being dragged out of bed by the ankles by an invisible pair of hands!

And it does not stop there. Sleep paralysis is also accompanied by hallucinations. You feel perfectly awake, eyes open, but frozen and it appears as though there are things happening in your room. Many people report seeing shadow people, supernatural creatures, ghosts, aliens, old witches and many other types of apparitions. The presence of the "entities" in the room is usually accompanied with some sort of a threat, physical attack, suffocation or a feeling of pressure on one's chest and difficulty breathing. So it's no wonder that a sleep paralysis episode is usually partnered with intense emotions of fear, horror, distress, panic and a fight-or-flight response. These are literally scenes out of the latest Hollywood horror film!

Universal experience

Sleep paralysis experiences have been suffered by humans across different cultures and historical timelines way before Hollywood and horror films ever existed. The Egyptians refer to it as a *Jinn* attack (*Jinn* are evil genies). For the Cambodians, it is known as "the ghost that pushes you down". Across the Caribbean, the local term for sleep paralysis is *kokma*. Among the Italians it is *pandafeche*, which refers to the evil witch, ghost or horrifying cat-like creature. In Japan, they call it *kanashibar*. In Newfoundland, it is known as "the old hag" who visits you in the night. In China, they know it as a "ghost oppression". It is no surprise that native folklore shapes the nature of sleep paralysis hallucinations.

In the US, it was only after the idea of flying saucers was popularized that people reported vivid alien abduction experiences, where aliens paralyzed and probed them in their beds at night. In Mexico, more than 90 per cent of teenagers know the phrase "a dead body climbed on top of me" to describe the nightmare entity. And in African culture, it is known as "the devil riding your back", where demons have sex with people in their sleep.

Even artists have depicted this ghoulish night-time disorder. The most recognized historical example of sleep paralysis is in the 1781 painting by Henry Fuseli called *The Nightmare*. The artwork is a classic depiction of the experiences of sleep paralysis, and shows the dreamer lying on her back and a small demon sitting on her chest.

Collective nightmares

It is interesting to note that people spanning history and various cultures all have in some way collectively experienced similar nightmares. Sometimes people collectively experience nightmares at the same time. When a society experiences collective trauma in the form of war, disease or natural disasters, it can produce a level of anxiety and emotional upset within the people as a whole. This can manifest itself in the form of collective nightmares, where people have similar anxiety-related nightmares.

Researchers at Tufts University in Massachusetts conducted a small study that looked at the dreams and nightmares of people after the 9/11 terror attacks in New York City. They wanted to see if the events produced some level of trauma to people in the US. After analysing the results of those involved in the study, they reported a marked increase in intense or vivid dreams and nightmares.

While writing this book, I was visiting my parents and engaged in conversation with my father about dreams. He told me that he had a recurring childhood nightmare of the Nazis coming to get him. The scene always involved trying to escape or hide from them and then being discovered or caught, and, just before he was to be killed, he woke up in fright. We discussed theories on why he might have had these recurring Nazi nightmares, and he came to the conclusion that it was most likely to do with the collective fear in America at the time. Having been born in 1937, my father was a small child during the trauma and atrocities of World War II, and at that time there was a lot of anxiety and fear in the world linked to it.

The collective shadow

With the collective nightmare comes the collective shadow. As with your own shadows that you reflect upon when analysing and decoding your own personal dreams and nightmares, the same can be done for the collective shadow. Jung often warned of the risk of "collective psychosis" in which whole societies would be engulfed by their suppressed shadow. If societies as a whole refuse to face their dark side, deny their inner work and dismiss responsibility for their subconscious behaviours, they might at some point boil over into irrational action.

Human beings appear to be in a loop of trauma, habitually repeating this trauma on themselves and others. By repeatedly re-enacting this trauma, much like the recurring dream, it would seem as though something is being shown to them. There is something to reflect on and to change. The question is whether society will be willing to see this and make the changes. Society has the opportunity either to transform or carry on in the collective trauma cycle.

Learning from your nightmares

Although there are many theories as to why you dream, they are ultimately a reflection of your unconscious and subconscious mind. As a conscious dreamer, you should embrace and acknowledge the guidance and messages from your inner dreamworld and seek to incorporate the positive, transformative aspects of them into your waking life. This, in turn, will enrich your soul, balance your wellbeing, and bring creativity and beauty into the world.

Hopefully it will also bring positive change into the world. As you shift your consciousness into the realms of connectivity, love, altruism and transcendence and shine this back out into the world, you can hopefully help society evolve as a whole away from repeated patterns of trauma, abuse and bad behaviour.

Rescripting your nightmares

Much like recurring dreams, there are a few techniques that you can incorporate into your conscious dreaming practice to transcend your nightmares. If you are able to achieve lucidity within the nightmare state, then even better, because you will be able to have the clarity of awareness to transform the outcome of the nightmare then and there.

Working through your nightmares will help you to work through your trauma, fears, emotional pain and anxiety, and face your shadow self.

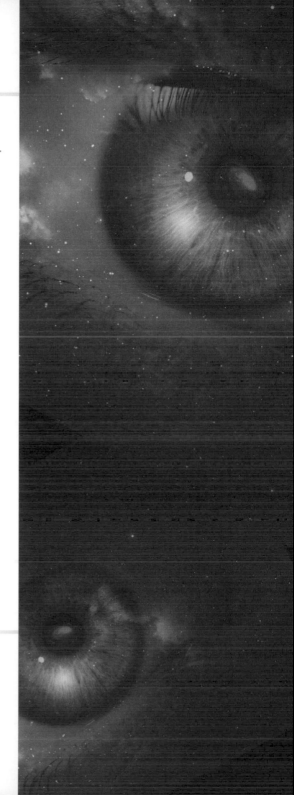

STEPS TO RESCRIPTING
YOUR NIGHTMARES

* Write down a nightmare that you can remember in your dream journal.

* Reflect on any dream symbols or abstractions.

* Analyse and decode the dream symbols or abstractions.

* Focus on the emotions within the nightmare.

* Analyse why you were afraid, terrified, anxious or disturbed.

* Write down your findings.

* Reflect on the precise moment of fear or terror in the nightmare scene.

* Imagine how you would change that moment.

* Write down this new version.

* Sit in quiet reflection and visualize the new positive and transformative version of the dream playing out in your mind's eye.

Lucid dreams

One of the most exciting, exhilarating and profound dreaming episodes that a conscious dreamer can hope to experience is per cent lucidity within a dream. A lucid dream is when the dreamer becomes fully aware that they are dreaming. They can then effectively navigate their dream environments with their conscious free will, control them to varying degrees and interact with dream characters in complete and vivid awareness.

Lucid dreaming dates back thousands of years, with accounts being recorded in an ancient Hindu tract called *Vigyan Bhairav Tantra.* The tract instructs how to best direct one's consciousness within dreams. Countless other cultures and traditions throughout history have also incorporated techniques and teachings that help the dreamer achieve lucidity within dreams. Although this unique dreaming experience has been around for centuries, It was not officially recognized by the scientific community until 1978.

Why lucid dream?

There is great potential in dreams. It is your inner space to explore the mystery of your conscious and your interconnectivity to the universe. Lucid dreams can bring mind-expanding, euphoric, deep, healing and mystical experiences to your journey. Achieving awareness in your dreams can help in working through emotional issues, taking control of nightmares, problem-solving, facing fears, curing phobias and bringing joy into your life.

CHARACTERISTICS OF A LUCID DREAM

To determine if you have been lucid dreaming, consider if your dreams have any of the following characteristics:

* Conscious and aware of yourself.

* Conscious of making decisions.

* Conscious of the dream environment and aware of the dream characters.

* Conscious of the meaning or symbolisms within the dream as they unfold.

* Aware of concentration and focus on tasks such as reading or problem-solving.

* Aware of memory functions and a clear memory of the waking world.

* Physical laws need not apply in the dream – you can fly, leap great distances, teleport.

* Details of the dream environment are vivid and clear.

* Your eyesight is vastly improved with 20/20 vision that is clear and vivid.

* Your senses such as touch, taste, smell and hearing are heightened.

Promoting lucid dreams

Through your conscious dreaming practice you can awaken your unconscious mind in your dreaming time and achieve lucidity. The key points of your conscious dreaming practice to help facilitate lucid dreams are:

HEALTHY SLEEP HYGIENE AND LIFESTYLE

The healthier your lifestyle and sleep hygiene (see page 32), the better your chances are at obtaining lucidity in your dreams. Lucidity is a connection and awareness within your mind, and you want to make sure you keep it in top shape. Regular and healthy sleep patterns, diet and lifestyle choices all have a direct effect on whether or not your dreaming time will be productive.

DREAM JOURNALING

The more you record your dreams (see page 76), the better your dream memory recall will become. Writing your dreams down also seems to trigger more dreams and helps keep you better connected to your dream realms. The dream brain muscle is one that you want to keep working out, and dream journaling is the optimum way of doing this. The practice of actively reflecting, embracing, deciphering and integrating your dreams into your waking life will result in a deeper connectivity to your dreams when they are actually occurring. This, in turn, will make your chances of becoming lucid in a dream much greater.

MINDFUL INTENT

Practising mindful intent daily (see page 59) will train your mind, awareness and consciousness to be present and observe. It is the zone that you want your brain to be able to access when you are in REM dream sleep (see page 26). It is the key to lucidity in a dream. If you are engaging in this mindfulness throughout the day, you will have a better chance of lucidity in your dreams. And, of course, do not forget to set your dream intent before you fall asleep. If you want a lucid dream, then set an intent for one.

DREAM SHARING

Much like dream journaling, engaging with other dreamers about your dreams (see page 96) will help to build your dream memory recall, trigger more dreams and effectively keep you closer to the dreaming realms. Dream sharing is also perfect for receiving advice, techniques and trying out dreaming experiments with other dream explorers.

DREAM HERBS

The dream herbs that you use in your conscious dreaming practice are also helpful in achieving lucidity. Although it is very understudied, it is thought that chemical compounds in dream plants such as mugwort and *Calea zacatechichi* are known to potentially trigger more vivid dreams, hypnagogic imagery or bring you into awareness within the dream. Engage in a Dream tea ritual (*see* page 86) before bed.

HYPNAGOGIC MEDITATION

Engaging in your daily hypnagogic meditation (*see* page 94) as part of your conscious dreaming practice will train your mind to observe the visuals within the dream state. It will also help you understand the visual language, symbols and metaphors of dreams without getting too emotionally caught up or attached to them.

RECOGNIZING DREAM GENRES

Understanding the variety of styles and genres of your dreams (*see* page 102) can assist in bringing awareness within the dream state: "Ah! This is a recurring dream!" Your dream genres are pieces of the puzzle. Being aware of all of the pieces will help you to fit them all together. This can help enormously when you are trying to achieve awareness and lucidity within your dreams.

Incorporating these key points of your conscious dreaming practice with an on-going commitment will help you to evolve and improve your dreaming abilities to the point where you can become a regular lucid dreamer.

TRICKING THE BRAIN TO LUCID DREAM

For hardcore experimentalists out there, an effective technique for encouraging lucid dreaming involves slightly altering your sleep pattern during the night. At the time of your sleep schedule when you should be experiencing REM sleep, you wake yourself up, which will stimulate your conscious mind. When you go back to sleep, you will slip into REM sleep, and because your conscious mind has already been activated it will be much easier to maintain that awareness when your REM dreams start to kick in.

To wake up during REM sleep and enhance your chances of lucid dreaming, follow these steps:

* Go to sleep at your usual scheduled time.

* Sleep for 4–5 hours and use an alarm to wake you up.

* Fully awaken yourself by doing a small task such as writing in your dream journal or getting up for a drink of water.

* Stay awake and alert for between 10 and 20 minutes.

* Go back to bed and relax.

* Set your intent to lucid dream.

* Observe your hypnagogic state.

* Use visualization to bring yourself back into your dream place.

* Fall into sleep.

* Lucid dream!

Staying in a lucid dream

You have finally been able to achieve lucidity in your dreams. However, once you become aware that you are dreaming, you get so excited that you wake up! This is a common experience for many oneironauts. The euphoria of achieving lucidity is just so powerful that it kicks people right out of the dream. Here are some ways in which you can keep yourself grounded within your lucid dream.

STAY CALM

When you get that initial rush of excitement of lucidity, do not get carried away. Immediately ground that energy. Literally, take hold of yourself and say, "Okay, chill out!" If you have been practising your mindful intent on a daily basis, this should be a lot easier because you will be more in touch with your calm and observant mind. Imagine the energy flowing back down through you into your feet, grounding you to the dream environment that you are in.

GET PHYSICAL

It can take a few tries to figure out what works for you. Perhaps staying calm is not the key. I know that for me it is very different. When I achieve lucidity in my dreams, I get massively hyperactive. I have almost got too much energy. Supercharged! So I need to do the opposite of staying calm. I need to embrace the hyper-energy to stay grounded within the dream. One way of doing this is to start spinning around quickly in your dream. Other physical activities can include jumping up and down really fast, clapping or waving your hands around, leaping, dancing or flying.

GET INSTRUCTIVE

For some dreamers using their clear and loud voice is enough to keep them grounded in their lucid dream. Shouting out statements of instruction and intent such as, "I ground myself in this dream!" can be enough to keep you there. You could even set yourself a task to stay within the dream by shouting out an instruction to yourself, such as, "I will fly over the ocean!" Find an instruction that you feel best suits you and stick to it. Your brain is more easily trained by the repetitive nature of the instructions you choose.

Mutual dreams

Have you ever experienced a dream of a relative or friend in which you were both doing a specific task, such as catching a train. Then the next day you hear from your relative or friend, who tells you that they also had a dream of you both catching a train? This is a mutual dream, and although it is not something that has been recognized fully by science, it is something that many people have reported experiencing.

So mutual dreams are when two (or more) people feature in each other's dreams and share the same dream environment. There might be slight variations in the details of each person's dream but the similarities can be uncanny.

Bonds between dreamers

Most mutual dreams are spontaneous and mysterious and can seem to indicate that a strong bond or emotional connection exists between the dreamers. There are a plethora of theories out there either to support or debunk mutual dreaming, including hoax, coincidence, telepathy, the collective unconscious, interconnectivity and quantum entanglement. The experiences and reports of mutual dreams raise the question that perhaps some type of information sharing is possible between people in the dream state.

Mutual dreams can be planned, meaning that two people actively work toward achieving one dream scenario or goal. It is a way to improve communication and build trust. Conscious dreamers who actively seek out mutual dreams see themselves as pioneers in this new territory.

Pairing up for mutual dreams

A conscious dreamer will usually want to explore, experiment and actively participate in this potentially interconnected space. However, most people are not conscious dreamers; they are unconscious dreamers. An unconscious dreamer probably has little or no development in this area of possibility.

If you are an advanced conscious dreamer or possess a lucid dreaming skill set and you pair up with someone of similar abilities, you will have the optimum conditions for the possibility of having mutual dreams. Mutual dreams between conscious and unconscious dreamers may be possible, but they will be more challenging.

MUTUAL DREAMING EXPERIMENT

If you want to experiment with mutual dreaming with a friend, loved one or relative, it is helpful to pair up with someone who shares the same sense of exploration, creativity and passion for dreaming as you and who is up for the experiment. Once you have found a mutual dream partner, you are ready to begin the experiment.

* Discuss the idea of the experiment and make a plan. For example: "Let's try to find each other in our dreams tonight."

* Set an intent before you fall asleep. For example: "I am going to find Zoe in my dreams tonight."

* Visualize making a connection with your friend. You can do this using your imagination, through visualization or through focused thought. For example: Visualize a swirling portal opening up to connect to your friend on the other side, or perhaps a door opening to your friend on the other side.

* Carry on with your intent and visualization into your hypnagogic state.

* Observe what takes shape in your hypnagogic imagery, maintaining the focused intent on connecting with your friend in your dreams.

* Slip into sleep.

Record your dreams in the morning in your dream journal. Writing down your dreams and sharing them with your mutual dreaming partner is the only way to gain feedback and confirmation of a mutual dream. Compare notes with your mutual dreaming friend to see what comes up. There may be uncanny similarities, slight similarities or absolutely none at all.

Embrace the explorative and pioneering spirit. Do not give up! Make it a practice to keep experimenting, setting goals and sharing with your mutual dreaming partner to see how things progress.

Precognitive dreams

One of the more mysterious aspects of dream exploration is the territory of precognition.

MY PRECOGNITIVE DREAM

On *23 December 2004*, as recorded in my personal dream journey, I had the following dream.

I dreamed I was in the Maldives with Adam. We were walking along the beach of a beautiful island. We looked out to sea and noticed there was no water left, only an empty sandy seabed. We saw islands off in the distance and decided to walk over to one of them across the seabed.

We reached one of the islands and a black woman came running over to us with a child in her arms. She had an American accent and a mixed-race child. She told us that we should get back to our island. She was frantic and told us that the water was going to come back when the moon was full.

All of a sudden, night fell and we noticed a full moon in the clear night sky. At that moment we heard a great roar and swooshing sound and the water came in huge waves, rolling over the dry seabed and crashing into the shore.

It was like a great huge wall, and when we walked from the shore, we could see that in the swooshing, rushing water there were hundreds of people and cars. We were then told by the African-American woman that we were stranded because the water damaged all the phone lines and internet.

Three days later on 26 December 2004, and notably on a full moon, the Indian Ocean earthquake and tsunami struck, killing approximately 280,000 people.

Dreaming of the future

The dream that I experienced is known as a precognitive dream. Also referred to as premonitory, psychic, prophetic, prescience, divinatory and future vision, these unusual dream experiences appear to predict the future.

The phenomenon of precognition does not align with the current established principles of science yet, despite this, many people still believe in it. Surveys show that up to 50 per cent of the general population report experiencing at least one precognitive dream.

Theories regarding precognition vary. The nonbelievers suggest memory bias, unconscious perception, coincidence, the law of large numbers and self-fulfilling prophecies, while the believers propose sixth sense, extrasensory perception, clairvoyance or interconnectivity to the collective unconscious.

BEARER OF GOOD NEWS

Precognitive dreams have a reputation for being omens or warnings about negative, ominous or destructive events, but not all of them are negative. Many people report having precognitive dreams that have predicted positive events, such as meeting a soulmate, the birth of a child, financial success or new inventions.

HOW TO RECOGNIZE A PRECOGNITIVE DREAM

There is actually no way you can tell if the dream you had is precognitive until that future event actually unfolds in waking life. So there is a conundrum here. However, there are some common traits that prophetic dreams end up having, after they are realized:

* Ultra-vivid dream scene that feels exceptionally real.

* Very high emotive content.

* A sense that, "This is going to happen."

* Random and out of the blue, not at all linked to anything or any drama in your waking life.

Exploring precognition

Precognitive dreams appear to be random and happen spontaneously, although there are people who claim that they are able to activate divinatory dreams through ritual and ceremony. If you find that you are prone to precognitive dreams, or that your exploratory mind is open to the possibilities of them, here is some advice on how to develop them.

BE AWARE

Begin to be consciously aware of your intuition and gut instinct when a precognitive dream is triggered. Be present with your inner voice and do not repress it. Write down reflections or take note of any premonitions or intuitive thoughts you experience during the day. Eventually, you will learn to trust yourself and your intuition, and your sensitivity will become second nature and in no way distressing.

BE RECEPTIVE

Synchronicities and signs might appear in your dreams and waking life as little precognitive prompts. Be open and receptive to them. They may also come to you in the forms of physical sensations or insights of feelings. Be sure to reflect upon them and record them in your dream journal. This will help you to build your receptivity as well as self-trust.

BE PRESENT

The fact that you may have experienced precognitive ability does not mean you need to be obsessive about the future. It is important to be in the present moment, free of fear and worry. If you are finding it challenging to stay present, spend more time with your mindful intent (see page 59), meditation practice (see page 94) or reflecting on these fears by writing them down. When you embrace the here and now, it will make you more grounded and receptive.

BE CALM

Sticking to your mindful intent throughout the day can help you to develop your inner calm, which will help you if your dreams appear to predict future events. The key is to not "freak out" when you see the events of one of your dreams unfold in waking reality. Remain calm and reflective and write in your dream journal about your feelings, insights and observations. The last thing you want to do is start making yourself feel fearful and "spooky" or shout out about it to all your friends for them to feel scared, too. Being intuitive and receptive is natural. The more you make the "supernatural" just "natural", the more calm, reflective and grounded you will be.

BE PROACTIVE

A committed dream journal practice can play a key role when experiencing precognitive dreams. A record of the dream, along with the date it occurred, can serve as proof that the dream was experienced before the event happened. This can be encouraging and reassuring for those developing their receptive abilities. Sitting in quiet reflection, either through mindful intent or meditation, is another proactive way to improve your receptiveness.

How can precognitive dreams help?

If precognitive dreams are a real thing and it is just a case that the current concepts of time and causality need updating, then why do human beings experience them in the first place and what is their purpose? It can be argued that those who possess precognitive abilities are nothing more than advanced empaths, highly intuitive individuals or people with heightened sensitivity. Like all things empathetic, it would appear that the function for possessing this sensitive quality is to simply help.

Precognitive information is like being told the weather forecast. Much like the weather, you can then decide your plan of action, to adapt to what is potentially coming. It can be an opportunity given to you to be aware of the possibilities of an outcome and navigate yourself to avoid a negative event or prepare you emotionally for a positive event.

The information can also be an opportunity for you to be more receptive to help those in need. For example, if you have a dream that your mother is diagnosed with an illness and has only a few months to live, then it could be a prompt for you to spend more time with her and show her your love.

Whatever the situation, do not freak yourself or other people out. Just because you had a dream that your friend died in a car accident does not mean that it will actually happen. Do not fall into the trap of superstitious thoughts. There is a delicate balance to be had, and it really comes down to the calm and grounded "knowing" of your intuition. There should be almost no emotional attachment to the insight. If all you experience is fear and obsessive thoughts, then it is most likely the fear loop of superstition.

FAMOUS PRECOGNITIVE DREAMS

There are some well-known cases of precognitive dreams by famous people. For example, in 1865, two weeks before Abraham Lincoln was shot dead, the US President had a precognitive dream about a funeral at the White House. In the dream, he asked someone to tell him who was in the casket and they replied, "the President of the United States." He told his wife about the dream but neither of them took it to heart. In fact, on the night of his assassination he gave his bodyguard the night off.

Another example is the American writer Mark Twain. He had a dream about his brother's corpse lying in a metal coffin in his sister's living room. It rested on two chairs, with a bouquet and a single crimson flower in the centre. He told his sister about his dream. Weeks later, his brother was killed in a massive explosion on a riverboat. Many others died and were buried in wooden coffins. But one onlooker felt such pity for young Henry that she raised the money for an expensive metal coffin. At the funeral, Twain saw the coffin as it was in his dream. As he stood over Henry's casket, a woman placed a bouquet with a single red rose in the middle.

After-death visitation dreams

One of the most unresearched and under-studied of all dream genres is the phenomenon of after-death visitation (ADV) dreams. In many of my dreaming circles and in the course of my work as a death doula, countless people have shared dreams in which they were visited by a deceased loved one or friend. The after-death visitation dreams that I have heard being shared and have researched all have similar qualities in the sense that they were healing and transformative, and they helped bring peace and solace to the grieving dreamer.

Whether you believe in an afterlife or not, there is no denying that an after-death visitation dream can bring comfort, emotional closure, peace and clarity to those experiencing loss and bereavement.

Universal experience

Over the span of history, humans have followed ancient traditions of honouring, respecting and seeking guidance from their dead ancestors. Ancestor worship is still practised all over the world. From the autumnal celebrations of Samhain in Ireland and Scotland to the vibrant *Dia de los Muertos* (Day of the Dead) in Mexico, people from all walks of life take the idea of their deceased loved ones seriously.

Characteristics of an after-death visitation dream

So what makes ADV dreams so special and how do we know if we have experienced one? The following list of characteristics will help you navigate and further understand this unique dreaming experience.

VIVID AND ULTRA-REALISTIC

The dream will feel like reality, and some dreamers become fully lucid within an after-death visitation dream. The dreamer will often note, "Wait a minute, my grandmother is dead. I must be dreaming!" Because of the clarity of awareness, it can make the dream much more profound, powerful, emotive and interactive.

SENSORY

Because the dream is hyper-vivid, and in some cases a lucid dream, sensations will be heightened. Your sense of touch and your olfactory senses might be activated. I have heard dreamers share accounts of holding their grandmother's hand or hugging their father and the tactile sensation feeling totally realistic. I have also heard accounts of dreamers smelling the perfume that was unique to their grandmother.

CALMING ENERGY

The energy of the dream is one of peace, love and sometimes joy.

TIMING

After-death visitations can occur out of the blue. Your loved one might have passed away 20 years prior to your dream and was not even on your mind. You could be having a standard dream and then all of a sudden they show up. Then there are after-death visitation dreams that occur shortly after the person has died.

THE DECEASED PERSON APPEARS YOUNGER

Another unusual attribute to after-death visitation dreams is that your deceased loved one appears to be a healthier and younger version of themselves.

CLARITY

The dream is not surreal, full of abstraction or confusing. It feels like a part of everyday life in many ways.

REASSURANCE

The deceased conveys a message of love, reassurance and joy. Messages are of the nature of, "I am doing well" or "I'll always be with you."

GUIDANCE

The deceased may also impart guidance, advice, reminders, insights, warnings or life wisdom. Some even joke around.

TELEPATHY

In other cases, the deceased communicates telepathically rather than verbally. Even without words, the dreamer is able to get the message.

CLOSURE

Many who have shared after-death visitation dreams have reported that the experience helped them with their grieving process. After integrating the dream, they felt like they had achieved closure and were able to cope better with the loss.

INTENSE EMOTIONS

Those who experience after-death visitation dreams often awaken feeling strong, usually experiencing positive emotions of love, joy, relief, astonishment or reflection.

MEMORABLE

An after-death visitation dream will stay with the dreamer for years. Because the dream is so vivid, emotive and profound, it is never forgotten.

TRANSFORMATIVE

One of the most prominent aspects of after-death visitation dreams is that they can completely transform the dreamer. Not only is it an emotional transformation, moving through and receiving closure during the grieving process, but it can also transform both the perspective and the consciousness of the dreamer. Many who have experienced after-death visitation dreams have noted a stronger interest in exploring existential questions, the bigger picture, and spiritual purpose and meaning.

Conclusion

It is a wonderful thing to explore, evolve and unfold the mystery that is your own mind. Like any expedition or exploration, it can be enriching, beautiful, empowering and enlightening, but it is not without its challenges. As a dream explorer, you can find yourself navigating through uncharted, shadowy territories and facing some of your deepest pains and fears. This can make you want to avoid the exploration because, like most people, you would rather just have magical, uplifting and positive dreams. But there is so much to glean even from your "not so positive" dreams. Nightmares, sleep paralysis, recurring dreams and anxious compensatory dreams all have something to teach you. Embrace these dreams with calmness, composure and reflection, and you may find that they become some of your biggest teachers.

Positive impacts on your life

Embracing a conscious dreaming practice will move you into an enriched and more connected dream life, as well as into a more enriched and deepened connection to self. You will begin to take notice of how this has a positive effect on your life and those around you.

You may find that your creative side bursts into life and is rich with ideas and inspiration. You may find that you begin to problem-solve and learn in your dreams, and that your dreams become a playground for you to acquire new insight. Or you may find that you begin to navigate and transcend past traumas or fears, embracing and overcoming nightmares and rescripting your recurring dreams.

Perhaps you will find yourself moving into a more sensitive interconnectivity with family, friends, loved ones, colleagues and acquaintances. You may begin to see the value of dreaming of people that you know, and begin to reflect on your interpersonal relationships or the symbolic archetypes that certain people can represent within the context of your dreams.

Conceivably, you may find that you develop a reconnection with nature, surrounding yourself with plants and being more mindful when outside observing and enjoying the natural world. You may even find you spend less time on your smartphone or at least become more disciplined as to how much time you spend on it.

You may also find that you begin to respect and honour your sleep time much more than in the past. As a result, you may begin to feel more aligned with your body and mind when it comes to restfulness and your sleep space.

You might even find that simply reading this book will trigger more dreams or help with your dream memory recall. It all starts with intent. The fact that you have this book in the first place means that you have already activated your journey into more connected dreaming!

One-third of our life is spent asleep and dreaming, which is around 25 years of unmapped terrain to explore. This is new terrain that we can actively navigate to help complement our waking experiences through this journey that we call life.

Tonight, as you lay your head to rest on your pillow, you can either nod off, count sheep, tune out or embrace the possibilities, adventures, inspiration and guidance of your dreams. I hope you feel inspired to join the exploration of YOU. See you in your dreams!

References

THE SCIENCE OF SLEEP

https://www.healthline.com/health/sleep-health/hypnagogic-hallucinations (accessed 15 August 2017)

Lachman, Gary, "Hypnagogia", *Fortean Times*, October 2002.

The stages of sleep

Aserinsky, E. & Kleitman, N. (1953), "Regularly occurring periods of eye mobility and concomitant phenomena during sleep", *Science*: 18, 273–4

Bonnet, M.H. (2011), "Acute sleep deprivation", in Kryger, M.H., Roth, T., Dement, W.C., eds., *Principles and Practice of Sleep Medicine*, 5th ed., Philadelphia: Elsevier Saunders: 54–66

Hauri, P. (1982), *Current Concepts: The Sleep Disorders*, 2nd Ed., Kalamazoo, MI: Upjohn Company

Huber, R., Esser, S.K., Ferrarelli, F., et al., "TMS-Induced cortical potentiation during wakefulness locally increases slow wave activity during sleep", PLOS ONE, http://journals.plos.org/plosone/article?id=10.1371/journal.pone.0000276

Rechtschaffen, A., Kales, A., eds. (1968), *A manual of standardized terminology, techniques, and scoring system for sleep stages in human subjects*, Los Angeles: Brain Information Service/Brain Research Institute, UCLA

"Stages of Sleep", Missouri University of Science *Psychology World* website, http://web.mst.edu/~psyworld/sleep_stages.htm

"The Sleep-Wake Cycle: Its Physiology and Impact on Health", National Sleep Foundation (2006), https://sleepfoundation.org/sites/default/files/SleepWakeCycle.pdf

Tononi, G, Cirelli, C. (2006), "Sleep function and synaptic homeostasis," *Sleep Med Rev.*: 10, 49–62

Brain waves

Buzsaki, György (2006). "Cycle 9, The Gamma Buzz", *Rhythms of the brain*, Oxford

Cantero, J.L., Atienza, M., Stickgold, R., Kahana, M.J., Madsen, J.R., Kocsis, B. (2003), "Sleep-dependent theta oscillations in the human hippocampus and neocortext", *J Neurosci*

"Glossary. A resource from the Division of Sleep Medicine at Harvard Medical School, Produced in partnership with WGBH Educational Foundation", Harvard University, 2008 Palva, S., Palva, J.M., (2007). "New vistas for a-frequency band oscillations", *Trends Neurosci.*, 30: 150–158

Zhang, Y., Chen, Y., Bressler, S.L., Ding, M. (2008), "Response preparation and inhibition: the role of the cortical sensorimotor beta rhythm", *Neuroscience*, 156 (1): 238–46.

SLEEP HYGIENE

de Biase et al., Eds. Garborino L.N. et al. (2014), "Sleep Hygiene", *Sleepiness and human impact assessment*, Springer, Milan

Gigli, G.L., Valente, M. (30 June 2012), "Should the definition of 'sleep hygiene' be antedated of a century? A historical note based on an old book by Paolo Mantegazza, rediscovered", *Neurological Sciences*, 34 (5): 755–60

Hirshkowitz, M,. Whiton, K. et al. (14 January 2015), "National Sleep Foundation's sleep time duration recommendations: methodology and results summary", *Sleep Health*, Elsevier Inc. 1 (1): 40–3

Howell, A. J., Dopko, R. L., Passmore, H., and Buro, K. (2011). "Nature connectedness: Associations with well-being and mindfulness", *Personality and Individual Differences*, 51, 166–71

Irish, L.A., Kline, C.E, Gunn, H.E, Buysse, D.J, Hall, M.H (October 2014), "The role of sleep hygiene in promoting public health: A review of empirical evidence", *Sleep Medicine Reviews*, 22: 23–36.

Luyster, F.S., Strollo, P.J., Zee, P.C., Walsh, J.K. (1 June 2012) "Sleep: A Health Imperative", *Sleep*

Wolverton, B.C., Douglas, W.L. Bounds, K. (July 1989), "A study of interior landscape plants for indoor air pollution abatement", NASA. NASA-TM-108061

Plants for improving air quality

Komori, T., Matsumoto, T., Motomura, E., and Shiroyama, T. (2006), "The sleep-enhancing effect of valerian inhalation and sleep-shortening effect of lemon inhalation", *Chemical Senses* 31, no. 8: 731–7

Kuratsune, H., Umigai, N., Takeno, R., Kajimoto, Y., and Nakano, T. (2010), "Effect of crocetin from Gardenia jasminoides Ellis on sleep: a pilot study", *Phytomedicine* 17, no. 11: 840–3

Sayorwan, W., Ruangrungsi, N., Piriyapunyporn, T., Hongratanaworakit, T., Kotchabhakdi, N., and Siripornpanich, V. (2012), "Effects of inhaled rosemary oil on subjective feelings and activities of the nervous system", *Scientia pharmaceutica* 81, no. 2: 531–42

Wolverton, B.C., and Wolverton, J. (1993), "Interior plants: Their influence on airborne microbes and relative humidity levels inside energy efficient buildings", *Res. Rep.* WES/100/05-93/001. Wolverton Environ. Serv., Inc. Picayune, Mississippi

Wolverton, B.C., and Wolverton, J. D. (1993), "Plants and soil microorganisms: removal of formaldehyde, xylene, and ammonia from the indoor environment", *Journal of the Mississippi Academy of Sciences*, 38, no. 2: 11–1

Yongchaiyudha, S., Rungpitarangsi, V., Bunyapraphatsara, N., andChokechaijaroenporn, O. (1996), "Antidiabetic activity of Aloe vera L. juice. I. Clinical trial in new cases of diabetes mellitus", *Phytomedicine* 3, no. 3: 241–3

THE FOUNDATIONS OF A CONSCIOUS DREAMING PRACTICE

Dream journaling

Read, J. (1995), *From Alchemy to Chemistry*, Dover, London, pp. 179–80

Dream plants and herbs

Akhondzadeh, S. (October 2001). "Passionflower in the treatment of generalized anxiety: a pilot double-blind randomized controlled trial with oxazepam", *Journal of Clinical Pharmacy and Therapeutics*, 26 (5): 363–367

Díaz, J.L. (1979), "Ethnopharmacology and taxonomy of Mexican psychodysleptic plants", *J Psychedelic Drugs*, 11(1–2), 71–101

Duenas, J., et al. (2016), "Amazonian Guayusa (Ilex guayusa Loes.): A Historical and Ethnobotanical Overview", *Economic Botany*, 70 (1): 85–91

"Food Patch Testing", Food Allergy Center, Massachusetts General Hospital, https://www.massgeneral.org/children/services/food-patch-testing.aspx (accessed 6 April 6 2014)

Johnson. C.P. (1862), *The Useful Plants of Great Britain: A Treastise*, Robert Hardwicke, London

Lewis, W.H., Kennelly, E.J., Bass, G.N., Wedner, H.J., Elvin, L. (1991), "Ritualistic use of the holly Ilex guayusa by Amazonian Jivaro Indians", *Journal of Ethnopharmacology*, 33: 25–30

Pollington, S. (2008), *Leechcraft: Early English Charms, Plantlore and Healing*, Anglo-Saxon Books

Par Kriminüllikuma spēkā stāšanās un piemērošanaз kartibu" (in Latvian), likumi.lv.

Rawson, J. (1984), *Chinese Ornament: The lotus and the dragon*, British Museum Publications; pp.200–2 (quoted)

Schultes, R.E. (1972), "Ilex guayusa from 500 AD to the present", in Wassén, H. et al., "A medicine-man's Implements and plants in a Tiahuanacoid tomb in highland Bolivia" Etnologiska Studier, 32, Goteborgs Etnografiska Museum

Simonienko, K., et al. (2013), "Psychoactive plant species – actual list of plants prohibited in Poland", *Psychiatria Polska*, XLVII(3), 499–508

Dream sharing

Krippner, St. Ed. (1990), *Dreamtime and Dreamwork: Decoding the Language of the Night (A New Consciousness)*, Jeremy P. Taracher, Inc.

Parkaman, S. (1990), *Dream and Culture. An Anthropological Study of the Western Intellectual Tradition*, Praeger Publishers

DREAM GENRES

Recurring dreams

Arnulf, I., Grosliere, L., Le Corvec, T., Golmard, J. L., Lascols, O., and Duguet, A. (2014), "Will students pass a competitive exam that they failed in their dreams?",

Consciousness and cognition, 29, 36–47

Barret, D. (2001), *Trauma and Dreams,* Harvard University Press

Davis, J. L., Byrd, P., Rhudy, J. L., and Wright, D.C. (2007), "Characteristics of chronic nightmares in a trauma-exposed treatment-seeking sample", *Dreaming,* 17(4), 187–98

Freud, S. (1950), *The Interpretation of Dreams*

Spoormaker, V. (2008), "A cognitive model of recurrent nightmares", *International Journal of Dream Research,* 1(1), 15–22

Wamsley, E. J., Tucker, M., Payne, J.D., Benavides, J.A., and Stickgold, R. (2010), "Dreaming of a learning task is associated with enhanced sleep-dependent memory consolidation", *Current Biology,* 20(9), 850–5

Zadra, A. (1996), "Recurrent dreams: Their relation to life events", in D. Barrett (ed.), *Trauma and dreams,* Cambride, MA, Harvard University Press

Lucid dreams

Holzinger, B. (2009), "Lucid dreaming – dreams of clarity", Contemporary Hypnosis, 26 (4): 216–224

Tholey, P. (1980), "Klarträume als Gegenstand empirischer Untersuchungen" (Conscious Dreams as an Object of Empirical Examination), *Gestalt Theory,* 2: 175–91

Tholey, P. (1980), "Empirisch Untersuchungen über Klarträume"(Empirical Examination of Conscious Dreams), *Gestalt Theory,* 3: 21–62

https://www.iamshaman.com/library/caleastudy.htm

Holzinger B (2009). "Lucid dreaming – dreams of clarity". *Contemporary Hypnosis.* 26 (4): 216–224. "DREAMING 2 (4) Abstracts – The Journal of the Association for the Study of Dreams"

Precognitive dreams

Bem, D. L. (2011), "Feeling the future: Experimental evidence for anomalous retroactive influences on cognition and affect", *Journal of Personality and Social Psychology,* 100, 407–25

Peake, A. (2012), *The Labyrinth of Time,* Arcturus, chapter 10 "Dreams and precognition"

Priestley, J.B. (1989), *Man and Time,* Aldus 1964, 2nd Ed., Bloomsbury

Ullman, M., Krippner, S., and Vaughan, A. (1989), "Dream telepathy: Experiments in nocturnal ESP", 2nd ed., Jefferson, NC, McFarland & Co.

After-death visitation dreams

Barrett, D. (1991), "Through a Glass Darkly: The Dead Appear in Dreams", *OMEGA: The Journal of Death and Dying*

Garfield, P. (2001), *Dreams in Bereavement From the Anthology Trauma and Dreams,* Harvard University Press

Krippner, S. and Faith, L. (2001), "Exotic Dreams: A Cross-Cultural Study Dreaming", *Journal of the Association for the Study of Dreams*

Shorter, J. E. (2010), "Visitation Dreams in Grieving Individuals: A Phenomenological Inquiry Into the Relationship Between Dreams and the Grieving Process", Institute of Transpersonal Psychology

Index

Picture credits

Alamy Stock Photo Piter Lenk 114-115; Sasin Paraksa 100-101. **Dreamstime.com** Corinna Gissemann 85. **Getty Images** © Marco Bottigelli 126-127; Lars Thulin 41; Rakop Tanyakam/EyeEm 30-31; sdominick 72; Yasuhide Fumoto 98-99. **iStock** 4X-image 100-101; AlasdairJames 37; anzeletti 27; Arndt_Vladimir 131; bingokid 67; Bogdan Khmelnytskyi 22-23; borchee 32-33; CatLane 58-59; chikaphotograph 51; deberarr 116-117; den-belitsky 128-129; Everste 132-133; ferrantraite 2; g-stockstudio 39; hippostudio 54; isabeltp 82-83; Matjaz Slanic 110-111; RuudMorijn 52-53, 119; Sidekick 42; solarseven 11; spooh 94; sssss1gmel 46-47; stock_colors 6-7. **Shutterstock** Africa Studio 45. **Unsplash** Adrian Pelletier 124-125; Chris Barbalis 102-103; Dan Grinwls 107; Denys Nevozhai 34-35; Frances Gunn 88; Gaelle Marcel 87; George Gvasalia 62; Jeremy Bishop 14-15; Joao Silas 74-75; Kyle Peyton 148; Laura Lefurgey Smith 56-57; Pablo Torres 18-19; Rod Sot 140-141; Sergey Pesterev 114-115; Steve Halama 96-97; Tobias Tullius 16; Todd Quackenbush 2.

Acknowledgements

Firstly, I would like to acknowledge all the amazing people who have worked with me on manifesting this book!

Kate Adams
Polly Poulter
Theresa Bebbington
Helen Ridge
MFE Editorial Services

Juliette Norsworthy
Ella McLean
Jennifer Veall
Giulia Hetherington
Lisa Pinnell

I also want to thank all the wonderful souls who have been pivotal throughout this journey, in both synchronistic and supportive ways. I am truly grateful for your presence.

The Lusterio Family
Adam Carr
Jan Carr
Susan Carr
Dan Nichols
Annette Nichols
Gonzalo & Delfina
Nissa & Fritz
Jenniffer ClarOscura
Kristina Florinda Estrellita
Sarah Janes
Charlie Morley
Jade Shaw
Sky Goodwin
Keith Ira Lorcain
Lorry Stone
Cat Dove
Karlie Shelley
Jen Dawson
Luis Solarat
Secret Yoga Club
The Grain Grocer

SonicSoul
Guerilla Science
D.Rem
Mar Mar
Magick
Margate Arts Club
David David
Michael Travis
Melissa Unger
Judy Nylon
Mangrey
Alejandro Castañeda Salinas
Jonah Emerson Bell
George Teal
Michele Occelli
Joan Stanger
Leslie Goosey
Serena Constance
Renata Spinelly Martins
Laura Nolan
Tina Solberg Torstad
John Rensten